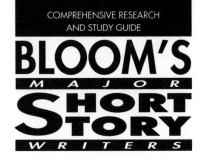

COMPREHENSIVE RESEARCH
AND STUDY GUIDE

BLOOM'S
MAJOR
SHORT
STORY
WRITERS

Jack

London

EDITED AND WITH AN
INTRODUCTION BY HAROLD BLOOM

CURRENTLY AVAILABLE

BLOOM'S MAJOR SHORT STORY WRITERS

Anton Chekhov

Joseph Conrad

Stephen Crane

William Faulkner

F. Scott Fitzgerald

Nathaniel Hawthorne

Ernest Hemingway

O. Henry

Shirley Jackson

Henry James

James Joyce

D. H. Lawrence

Jack London

Herman Melville

Flannery O'Connor

Edgar Allan Poe

Katherine Anne Porter

J. D. Salinger

John Steinbeck

Mark Twain

John Updike

Eudora Welty

BLOOM'S MAJOR WORLD POETS

Maya Angelou

Robert Browning

Geoffrey Chaucer

Samuel T. Coleridge

Dante

Emily Dickinson

John Donne

T. S. Eliot

Robert Frost

Homer

Langston Hughes

John Keats

John Milton

Sylvia Plath

Edgar Allan Poe

Poets of World War I

Shakespeare's Poems & Sonnets

Percy Shelley

Alfred, Lord Tennyson

Walt Whitman

William Wordsworth

William Butler Yeats

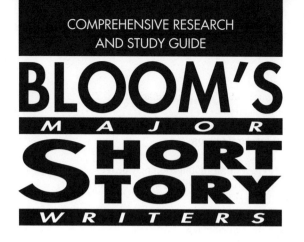

COMPREHENSIVE RESEARCH
AND STUDY GUIDE

BLOOM'S
MAJOR
SHORT
STORY
WRITERS

Jack
London

BLOOM

First Printing
1 3 5 7 9 8 6 4 2

Library of Congress Cataloging-in-Publication Data
Jack London / edited and with an introduction by Harold Bloom.
    p. cm. — (Bloom's major short story writers)
    Includes bibliographical references (p.) and index.
    ISBN 0-7910-5945-6 (alk. paper)
    1. London, Jack, 1876–1916—Criticism and interpretation—
Handbooks, manuals, etc. 2. London, Jack, 1876–1916—
Examinations—Study guides. 3. Short story—Examinations—
Study guides. 4. Short story—Handbooks, manuals, etc.
I. Bloom, Harold. II. Series.
PS3523.O46 Z648   2001
813'.52—dc21   023095

Chelsea House Publishers
1974 Sproul Road, Suite 400
Broomall, PA 19008-0914

The Chelsea House World Wide Web address is
http://www.chelseahouse.com

Contributing Editor: Erica DaCosta

Produced by: Robert Gerson Publisher's Services, Santa Barbara, CA

Contents

User's Guide

This volume is designed to present biographical, critical, and bibliographical information on the author's best-known or most important short stories. Following Harold Bloom's editor's note and introduction is a detailed biography of the author, discussing major life events and important literary accomplishments. A plot summary of each short story follows, tracing significant themes, patterns, and motifs in the work, and an annotated list of characters supplies brief information on the main characters in each story.

A selection of critical extracts, derived from previously published material from leading critics, analyzes aspects of each short story. The extracts consist of statements from the author, if available, early reviews of the work, and later evaluations up to the present. A bibliography of the author's writings (including a complete list of all books written, cowritten, edited, and translated), a list of additional books and articles on the author and the work, and an index of themes and ideas in the author's writings conclude the volume.

~

Harold Bloom is Sterling Professor of the Humanities at Yale University and Henry W. and Albert A. Berg Professor of English at the New York University Graduate School. He is the author of over 20 books, including *Shelley's Mythmaking* (1959), *The Visionary Company* (1961), *Blake's Apocalypse* (1963), *Yeats* (1970), *A Map of Misreading* (1975), *Kabbalah and Criticism* (1975), *Agon: Toward a Theory of Revisionism* (1982), *The American Religion* (1992), *The Western Canon* (1994), and *Omens of Millennium: The Gnosis of Angels, Dreams, and Resurrection* (1996). *The Anxiety of Influence* (1973) sets forth Professor Bloom's provocative theory of the literary relationships between the great writers and their predecessors. His most recent books include *Shakespeare: The Invention of the Human*, a 1998 National Book Award finalist, and *How to Read and Why*, which was published in 2000.

Professor Bloom earned his Ph.D. from Yale University in 1955 and has served on the Yale faculty since then. He is a 1985 MacArthur Foundation Award recipient, served as the Charles Eliot Norton Professor of Poetry at Harvard University in 1987–88, and has received honorary degrees from the universities of Rome and Bologna. In 1999, Professor Bloom received the prestigious American Academy of Arts and Letters Gold Medal for Criticism.

Currently, Harold Bloom is the editor of numerous Chelsea House volumes of literary criticism, including the series BLOOM'S NOTES, BLOOM'S MAJOR DRAMATISTS, BLOOM'S MAJOR NOVELISTS, MAJOR LITERARY CHARACTERS, MODERN CRITICAL VIEWS, MODERN CRITICAL INTERPRETATIONS, and WOMEN WRITERS OF ENGLISH AND THEIR WORKS.

Editor's Note

My Introduction discusses Jack London's continued appeal to readers of all ages, finding that his short stories and some of the episodes from his novels transcend the novels themselves.

As there are some 22 essays excerpted here, I will confine my comments to those I find most enlightening. The noted critic Maxwell Geismar comments on two episodes from London's novels, "For the Love of a Man" from *The Call of the Wild* and "The She-Wolf" from *White Fang*. Charles N. Watson Jr. compares *The Call of the Wild* to *Huckleberry Finn*, while Donald Pizer compares *White Fang* and *The Call of the Wild*.

Franklin Walker and James I. McClintock find socialism/Marxism to have influenced London's fiction in their analysis of "The Apostate."

In the volume's final essay, James Mellard explains the mythical overtones of "To Build a Fire" (1908), perhaps London's best-known short story. ❀

Introduction

HAROLD BLOOM

Jack London died at forty in 1916, possibly of a drug overdose. An auto-didact, the self-named Jack London worked as an oyster pirate, a seaman, a power plant laborer, but was most himself as a vagrant and a revolutionary, until he became a professional writer, and then a war correspondent. A voyager, rancher, Socialist politician, a permanent adventurer, an incessant writer: London's energies were beyond measure. He remains both a phenomenon of our imaginative literature and a permanent figure in the American mythology.

His best stories—including "To Build a Fire" (1908), "The She-Wolf," "For the Love of a Man," and "The Apostate"—surpass his novels and fantasies in literary power. The realism of the stories is so extreme and intense that they border upon hallucinatory phantasmagorias. Dogs transmute into wolves, if they are not eaten by wolves, and men struggle lest they themselves be devoured. Death is everywhere in Jack London's Klondike: freezing, starvation, wolves fuse into a composite menace.

The Call of the Wild (1903) opens with a section called "Into the Primitive" which is a fair motto for Jack London's literary quest. Here I want to center upon "The She-Wolf," the second story or episode in *White Fang* (1906). London's grim sense of determinism haunts the entire book, whose opening section "The Trail of the Meat," sums up the metaphysic of the work:

> It is not the way of the Wild to like movement. Life is an offence to it, for life is movement; and the Wild aims always to destroy movement. It freezes the water to prevent it running to the sea; it drives the sap out of the trees till they are frozen in their mighty hearts; and most ferociously and terribly of all does the Wild harry and crush into submission man—man, who is the most restless of life, ever in revolt against the dictum that all movement must in the end come to the cessation of movement.

Jack London writes in the interval between Schopenhauer's analysis of the Will to Live and Freud's uncanny apprehension that the inanimate is our destination and origin, the vision of *Beyond the Pleasure Principle*. Yet London, though he gives the Wild his allegiance, retains a kind of last-ditch humanism. Bill and Henry, hunted by the wolf-pack, "two men who were not yet dead," are marked by the dignity of their mutual regard and their desperate courage. Down to three bullets and six sled-dogs, they are vastly outnumbered by the wolves. Their particular nemesis is the she-wolf, a husky sled-dog gone back to the Wild, and now a leader of the wolf-pack.

In the next episode, Bill joins the dogs as the she-wolf's victim, and Henry is a solitary survivor. It is London's peculiar power that his empathy extends equally to the she-wolf and to her human antagonists. Among writers of children's literature, London's stance would be more commonplace. I cannot think of a full analogue, in adult popular literature, to London's affinity for animals except for Kipling, who so beautifully blurs the line between the child's and the adult's imagination. Kipling was a far more versatile and gifted writer than Jack London, and had nothing in him of London's savage primitivism. But that worship of the Wild still marks London's difference from nearly everyone else, and accounts for London's permanent appeal to readers throughout the world. ❀

Biography of
Jack London

Jack London was born in San Francisco on January 12, 1876. His given name was John Griffith Chaney, but as he was growing up, his family called him Johnny. To the rest of the world, he was Jack.

His mother, Flora Wellman Chaney, married John London when Jack was eight months old. John London was a widower with two daughters, Ida and Eliza, and Jack probably did not know John London was not his real father until Jack was 21. At that point, Jack began searching for information on his birth father. William Henry Chaney, an astrologer and lecturer, had left his mother before Jack was born because Flora refused to destroy her unborn child. Flora was so depressed afterward that she attempted suicide twice in two days. When Jack eventually contacted his birth father, Chaney denied in several letters that he had ever been married to Flora, and he refused to acknowledge that he was Jack's father.

In some ways, Jack's childhood was not an easy one. Flora showed little love to the son she saw as her shame. She did, however, expect him to contribute to the family income as soon as he was old enough. Throughout her life, she was emotionally unstable; family members attributed her mental imbalance to a high fever in her childhood.

Luckily, John London, Jack's stepfather, was a kind and gentle man, and he loved Jack as his own son. They were very close, and Jack's stepsister Eliza acted as a kind of stepmother to him. She married and left home when she was sixteen, however, when Jack was still under ten.

Flora was an ambitious woman who pushed her husband continually to do bigger and better things. Her drive apparently worked for a while, for at one point, when Jack was about nine, the family owned an 87-acre ranch. Eventually, though, every money-making scheme failed, and for the majority of Jack's growing-up years, the family was poor.

From an early age, Jack loved to read, and he read nearly constantly, whatever he could get his hands on, no matter what it was. As he grew older, though, he had less time for reading, for he was expected to contribute to the family's income.

His first job was as a newspaper carrier. Every cent he earned went to help buy his family's food. After he graduated from grammar school in 1889, he went to work at Hickmott's Cannery. A full day's work there was 12 hours, but he often worked 18-hour shifts, with only a half-hour break for lunch and half an hour for supper. He made ten cents an hour, and again, everything went to his mother. Once, however, he tried to keep out enough money to buy a small rowboat, which cost eight dollars. He scrimped and saved, still turning most of his money over to his mother. When he had saved five dollars, his mother came to the cannery and demanded the money, which he was obliged to give her.

While he was working at the cannery, he saw little children as young as six or seven doing the same job he was. This injustice made a great impression on him and helped turn him to socialism later.

When he was fifteen, he borrowed some money to buy a boat, a sloop called the *Razzle Dazzle,* and became an oyster pirate, raiding the oyster beds at night and selling the oysters the next morning. (The raiding was a felony.) He lived aboard the boat and became known as "Prince of the Oyster Pirates." He later said he made more money in a week as an oyster pirate than he had in a year at the cannery. One day, however, he read a newspaper article about a pirate getting caught; he began having second thoughts about his career.

Jack then became a deputy fish patrolman with the San Francisco Bay Fish Patrol. He didn't actually have a salary now, but he did get half the fines from the fishermen he arrested. In the fall of 1892, he quit this job for two reasons: the fish patrolmen drank a lot, and he was beginning to drink much more heavily than he should—and he wanted to see the rest of the world.

In 1893 he joined the crew of the *Sophia Sutherland.* The ship was a sealing schooner that took him on an eight-month expedition to places as far away as Hawaii, Siberia, and Japan. He wrote about his experiences in an essay titled "Story of a Typhoon off the Coast of Japan," which won first prize ($25) in a San Francisco newspaper contest.

Jack next worked at a jute mill in Oakland, again earning ten cents an hour. The job was easy—all he had to do was wind the jute twine from spinning large bobbins onto smaller ones—but the work was drudgery, and Jack hated it. Finally, he quit when the owners of the mill refused to raise his pay.

Then he became a coal heaver, with a salary of thirty dollars a month. A coal heaver's position was the bottom of the ladder at a power plant, but Jack had been told he would be able to move up. He discovered, however, that he had been hired to replace two men who had been making forty dollars a month each. Furious at this discovery, he quit.

He planned on marching on Washington with Kelley's Army to protest unemployment, but halfway across the country with the rest of the "army" he decided he couldn't stand the conditions, especially the lack of food, and so he abandoned this cause. Instead, he rode a boxcar up to Chicago and then to Niagara Falls. Here, he was arrested for vagrancy and spent 30 days in jail. He returned to Oakland via train through Canada and then by ship from Vancouver, working his way home on a coal stoker.

Upon his return to Oakland, Jack became determined to become a writer. He continued his education at Oakland High School, working odd jobs to help out with rent and food. He finished high school and attended the University of California for just over one semester. Unfortunately, financial difficulties forced him to abandon his education.

In 1897, he joined the Klondike Gold Rush and went north with his brother-in-law, Eliza's husband. Shortly after their departure, John London, who had not been well for some time, died.

In Alaska, Jack spent time on the Dyea Trail, the trail he later wrote about in *The Call of the Wild*. The conditions were hard, and Captain Shepard, Jack's brother-in-law, lasted two days on the trail before turning around and going home. In the spring of 1898, Jack became ill with scurvy, and he too had to return to Oakland, as there was no treatment for the disease available in the North.

He began writing about his Northland experiences, and in 1889 he was published in the *Atlantic Monthly* magazine. The short story called "An Odyssey of the North" was his literary breakthrough. He was also published in the *Overland Monthly* ("To the Man on the Trail").

As a result of his publication success, London became famous locally. His fame brought him little advantages, however. Mostly, it meant that his old shipmates looked him up to ask for money.

Around 1900, Jack began spending a lot of time with Bessie Maddern. He liked her and respected her, but he did not love her. Her fiancé had recently died, and she did not care that Jack did not love her, as she did not love him either; when he asked her to marry him, she assumed they would fall in love with each other eventually. Their decision to marry was an impulsive one on both their parts; Jack proposed one night, and they were married the next Saturday (April 7, 1900). Although Bessie did fall very much in love with Jack, he never did return the feeling. They were extremely different types of people with almost nothing in common. By the fall of that year, though, Bessie was pregnant. Their daughter Joan was born on January 15, 1901.

Jack looked for comfort elsewhere. He had met the Russian socialist lecturer Anna Strunsky in 1899, and for years they carried on a correspondence. They wrote about socialism, of course, but also about such things as love. They were not in love at first, but in 1902, Jack began to fall in love with her. Anna did not reciprocate, and nothing came of Jack's feelings. His correspondence with Anna did make him more unhappy with his marriage, though, as he realized that marriage between two people who truly loved each other would be more fulfilling than what he had.

In the meantime, London became more and more involved in the local socialist party. In 1901, he ran for mayor of Oakland for the Social Democrat party. He received only 245 votes, but his aim had not been an election but publicity for the party, which he had accomplished.

Jack and Bessie's second daughter, Bess (later called Becky), was born October 20, 1902, while Jack was in Europe researching a book on the sociological conditions of London's East End. About this time, he decided he wanted to make his marriage work. He resolved to put more effort into his relationship with Bessie.

Despite his good intentions, however, he began to realize that his marriage to Bessie was not going to work; things were becoming more and more difficult between them. Frustrated, he fell in love with Charmian Kittridge and she with him. (Several months before his marriage to Bessie, Jack had met Charmian; a few months later, he asked her out on a date—a date he broke because he and Bessie were getting married that day.)

In January 1904, London sailed for Japan to cover the Russo-Japanese War for the Hearst syndicate. The correspondents were not able to get anywhere near the action, and therefore they had little chance of getting any interesting information. Frustrated and disgusted, London eventually went home.

In June 1904, Bessie filed for divorce on the grounds of desertion. Although Anna Strunsky was not accused of doing anything wrong, she was listed as one of the causes of the separation, as Bessie was aware of Jack and Anna's correspondence. Bessie was granted the divorce in November, which meant it would become final a year later.

On November 19, 1905, one day after his divorce from Bessie was finalized, Jack married Charmian. Their action shocked the American people, but Jack and Charmian didn't care; they were happy in everything they did together. Charmian realized that by marrying Jack she was marrying his writing as well, but she loved both Jack and his work. They took a honeymoon in Jamaica, leaving at the end of December after Jack had completed a lecture tour. They were happy together until Jack's death.

Early in 1906, London began to have a boat built, named the *Snark* after Lewis Carroll's *The Hunting of the Snark*. The construction cost much more than he had anticipated, due to the increased cost of materials after the San Francisco earthquake and fire. The *Snark* was finished at last, and on April 23, 1907, Jack, Charmian, and their crew left on a voyage they hoped would take them all over the world. They intended their journey to last seven years, but after the first leg of their trip—to Hawaii—they discovered that the boat leaked. The crew fell apart, going one way and another, and Jack and Charmian spent five months in Hawaii, taking short trips around the islands. They continued to have troubles with the boat—both with finding a reliable crew and having repairs done—but eventually, the boat was fixed. The Londons sailed through the South Sea Islands to New Zealand and Australia, while Jack wrote and gathered material for more writing, as he had been doing for much of his life.

In June of 1910, Charmian entered an Oakland hospital to give birth to their first child. The birth was difficult, and after little more than a day, the baby girl died. They had named her Joy, and her death nearly crushed them.

The *Snark* was sold in the fall of 1910 for much less than its cost. Soon, though, Jack bought a boat called the *Roamer*. This boat was much smaller than the *Snark*, and the Londons used it to make short trips around the San Francisco Bay, spending much of their time on the water. Jack found that sailing helped him to overcome the depression he suffered after Joy's death.

Besides his ongoing love of boats, Jack's favorite sport was boxing. He sparred with Charmian, his favorite partner, nearly every day. He also worked as a boxing reporter several times during his life.

In January 1912, the Londons were in New York. When the time came to return to the West Coast, they signed on to a ship with Jack as third mate and Charmian as stewardess. The *Dirigo* was traveling from New York to Seattle around Cape Horn, and Jack wanted to gather material for a novel from this voyage.

During the voyage, however, he apparently contracted a tropical sickness while in the Solomon Islands. Then, in 1913, he had appendicitis, and doctors discovered that his kidneys were diseased. This was a bad year for him: his nephew was nearly electrocuted, one of his horses was accidentally killed, frost killed his fruit crop, locusts ate his eucalyptus trees, hot wind scorched his corn, his house burned down—and all this was on top of his health problems.

London had drank heavily at several points in his life, but now, his doctors told him, he had to stop drinking completely. Even if he abstained from alcohol, however, both Jack and his doctor knew he had only a few years left to live. Jack did not tell anyone else, however. Instead, he continued with his travels and writing.

But his health continued to deteriorate. While trying to report on the Mexican Revolution, he contracted dysentery. His physical condition was further weakened by chronic uremia (a complication caused by kidney failure). In the fall of 1916, he became very sick and on November 22, at age 40, he went into a coma and died.

Many people attended his funeral. He was cremated and his ashes were buried on the ranch where he and Charmian had lived. A huge boulder was rolled over the grave as he had requested.

During his lifetime Jack London was often accused of plagiarism, since he mixed his personal experiences with the stories of others. He never bothered denying that he had used these sources (he even bought some plots from other authors), but he said that although he didn't seem to be very good at creating, he was very good at elaborating. Plots were hard for him, but he loved to express his ideas in writing. He wrote prolifically for 20 years—over 200 short stories, 20 novels, 400 nonfiction pieces, and 3 plays. His reputation today, however, is based mainly on the works he set in the North Country: 28 short stories, 4 novels, 6 non-fiction pieces, and a single play. Despite his artistic flaws, his fiction continues to endure. ❀

Plot Summary of
"For the Love of a Man"

The story is a part of *The Call of the Wild*, a novel that opens in the fall of 1897, during the Klondike gold rush. Buck, the protagonist, is a dog, a St. Bernard and Scotch Shepherd mix, who originally lived on an estate in the Santa Clara valley in California. There he had the run of the place, ruling over all the other estate dogs.

However, he is stolen from his easy life and finds himself instead living the life of a sled dog in the North. He comes to realize that this is a new place with new rules, and that he must learn these rules to survive. He becomes cunning and secretive in order to live. His body also toughens up quickly in the difficult conditions. His instincts become sharpened and the memories of his ancestors stir within him, so that he instinctively knows things without having personally experienced them.

Buck and his teammates pass through several hands, and they are treated cruelly by their owners. At last, weak and starving, Buck encounters John Thornton, who has a camp at the mouth of the White River. When Buck is beaten by his owner, John Thornton steps in and saves the dog. The other dogs and their owners fall through the ice to their deaths, leaving Buck with Thornton.

John Thornton takes good care of Buck. Thornton is himself recovering from frostbitten feet, and the two recover together. Buck makes friends with Thornton's other two dogs, Skeet and Nig, especially Skeet, a little Irish Setter who takes it upon herself to nurse Buck back to health. Buck is overwhelmed by Thornton's kindness, and for the first time in his life he feels real love for a man; not only has Thornton saved his life, he is also a near perfect master.

Although Buck adores Thornton, he does not become civilized again. The wildness has awoken in him and it remains. Even while he is with Thornton, he is called by his renewed instincts and the memories of his ancestors. His loyalty to Thornton is the only thing that keeps him from setting off on his own into the wild. Thornton is awed and a little frightened by the extent of Buck's devotion to him, especially one day when, on a whim, Thornton tells Buck to jump over a cliff, and then has to leap after the dog to keep him from really going over.

Buck continues to prove his love for Thornton. He fights off Black Burton, a man in a bar who attacks Thornton, and Buck later saves Thornton's life when in the rapids their boat capsizes. Thornton is flung out, and Buck leaps in after him and eventually pulls him to safety.

One evening that winter, Thornton brags to some men that Buck can pull a thousand pounds for a hundred yards, plus break the sled out of the ice first. One of the other men there bets a thousand dollars that Buck can't live up to Thornton's boasts. Thornton's bluff is called; he doesn't even have a thousand dollars, and so he is forced to borrow it in case he loses. When the men go outside and look at the sled loaded with twenty 50-pound sacks of flour, they up the wager to sixteen hundred dollars.

Buck meets the nearly impossible challenge and wins John Thornton the money. He achieves this feat because of his great love for the man. ❈

List of Characters in
"For the Love of a Man"

Buck is the protagonist, a St. Bernard–Scotch Shepherd cross; he is a 140-pound dog who grew up pampered on a California ranch until he was kidnapped and taken up North to be a sled dog.

John Thornton saves Buck's life and in return Buck feels bound to him. Thornton is kind and generous, and Buck loves him as he has never loved anyone before. Buck repeatedly saves Thornton's life and wins him sixteen hundred dollars.

Skeet is a female dog who also belongs to John Thornton. She is motherly toward Buck.

Nig is another dog belonging to John Thornton.

Black Burton is a man in a bar who attacks John Thornton. ❈

Critical Views on
"For the Love of a Man"

MAXWELL GEISMAR ON LONDON'S DOG PSYCHOLOGY

[This excerpt is from Maxwell Geismar's book *Rebels and Ancestors: The American Novel, 1890–1915*. In it, Geismar deals with the psychology of dogs as portrayed by Jack London.]

One notices how delicately London kept his story within the limits of credible animal behavior. The human beings are good or bad, efficient or useless, only to the degree that they affect the well-being of the dogs—and here indeed the brutes often rose to a stoic dignity not granted to the humans. There was the death of Curly as the huskies rush her and she is lost beneath the bristling mass of bodies ("So that was the way. . . . Once down, that was the end of you.") or the description of So-leks, a one-eyed battler, very Hemingwayish, who "asked nothing, gave nothing, expected nothing." There was Dave, the dog who fell sick but refused to relinquish his place in the team until he was driven away and shot; and the brief, sparkling scene when Buck first learns how to sleep, completely buried in a warm, snug ball under the Alaska snow.

An excellent passage described Buck's first act of theft, "the decay . . . of his moral nature . . . in the ruthless struggle for existence,"—a favorite theme, as we know, in the naturalism of the 1900's, and more convincing at times in a canine hero than in a dentist or financier. From Stephen Crane and Frank Norris, too, the novels of the time were filled with the howls, oaths, imprecations of heroes who harkened back to primitive epics—this was a noisy literature—just as here the song of the huskies, "with the aurora borealis flaming coldly overhead, or the stars leaping in the frost dance, and the land numb and frozen under its pall of snow," was "one of the first songs of the younger world in a day when songs were sad." Thus Buck learned to kill and to defend himself:

> It was no task for him to learn to fight with cut and slash and the quick wolf snap. In this manner had fought forgotten ancestors. They quickened the old life within him, and the old tricks which they stamped into the heredity of the breed were his tricks. They came to

him without effort of discovery, as though they had been his always. And when, on the still cold nights, he pointed his nose at a star and howled long and wolf-like, it was his ancestors, dead and dust, pointing nose at a star and howling down through the centuries and through him.

And so London carried us back—with an ease and sureness of perception that appeared also to be "without effort of discovery"—through the ages of fire and roof to the raw beginnings of animal creation. . . . The theory of racial instinct, of memory as inherited habit, that was at the start, through long aeons, a very conscious and alert process of behavior indeed—this theory, as developed by such figures as Samuel Butler, Bergson or Jung, was very clear here, of course. Similarly, the scene in which Buck finally deposed Spitz as the leader of the team, surrounded by the ring of huskies waiting to kill and eat the vanquished king, was a perfect instance of the 'son-hoard' theory which Frazer traced in *The Golden Bough,* and of that primitive ritual to which Freud himself attributed both a sense of original sin and the fundamental ceremony of religious exorcism. But what is fascinating in *The Call of the Wild* is the brilliance of London's own intuitions (quite apart from any system of psychology) in this study of animal instincts which are the first, as they are the final biological response to the blind savagery of existence.

If London's portraits of twentieth century supermen almost always sound fabricated and false, this legend of the super-brute— the dominant primordial beast—was completely natural, delicate and even tragic in the purlieu of a dog world and its flickering reflections of the buried night-life of the race. And there was another theme that became a favorite in the 1920's. The shifting, tortuous relationship of the hunter and the hunted had its roots also in this instinctive Darwinian cosmos. Indeed, when the memories of his heredity that gave, in Buck's eyes, a seeming familiarity to things he had never seen before are fully quickened and alive again, he experienced in the joy of the kill itself "an ecstasy that marks the summit of life, and beyond which life cannot rise." The moment of impending death was the moment of life at its most intense pitch, when London's hero, too, was sounding the deeps of his nature, and those strains, deeper than he, which went back to the womb of life. "He was older than the days he had seen and the breaths he had drawn. He linked the past with the present and eternity throbbed through him in a mighty rhythm to which he swayed as the tides and seasons swayed." And the underlying structure of dream and myth in *The Call of the Wild* was summarized, of course, in the final episode where all the premonitions of 'the trap' in this primordial world—and of those "wayfarers to death" in an earlier episode of the story—were more than justified.

> —Maxwell Geismar, "Jack London: The Short Cut: The False Dawn," *Rebels and Ancestors: The American Novel, 1890–1915* (Cambridge: Riverside Press, 1953): pp. 149–51.

⊗

CHARLES CHILD WALCUTT ON POINT OF VIEW IN *THE CALL OF THE WILD*

[This excerpt is from Charles Child Walcutt's chapter "Jack London: Blond Beasts and Supermen" from his book *American Literary Naturalism, A Divided Stream.* Here, Walcutt discusses point of view in *The Call of the Wild.*]

By Chapter III, Buck is "The Dominant Primordial Beast"; and the story proceeds as the conflict for mastery between Buck and Spitz, the treacherous and hated lead-dog of the team. "It was inevitable that the clash for leadership should come. Buck wanted it. He wanted it because it was his nature, because he had been gripped tight by that nameless, incomprehensible pride of the trail and trace—that pride which holds dogs in the toil to the last gasp, which lures them to die joyfully in the harness, and breaks their hearts if they are cut out of the harness." Spitz is experienced. Buck is intelligent and big; he has imagination, and his prowess increases. Always it is the life-impulse in him expressing itself. London pauses in a muscle-flexing digression to explain the nature of this impulse:

> There is an ecstasy that marks the summit of life, and beyond which life cannot rise. And such is the paradox of living, this ecstasy comes when one is most alive, and it comes as a complete forgetfulness that one is alive. This ecstasy, this forgetfulness of living, comes to the artist, caught up and out of himself in a sheet of flame; it comes to the soldier, war-mad on a stricken field and refusing quarter; and it came to Buck, leading the pack, sounding the old wolf-cry,

straining after the food that was alive and that fled swiftly before him through the moonlight. He was sounding the deeps of his nature, and of the parts of his nature that were deeper than he, going back to the womb of Time. He was mastered by the sheer surging joy of life, the tidal wave of being, the perfect joy of each separate muscle, joint, and sinew in that it was everything that was not death, that it was aglow and rampant, expressing itself in movement, flying exultantly under the stars and over the face of dead matter that did not move.

This is the materialistic philosophy transformed by the celebration of the single vital and inescapable fact which even materialism recognizes as valuable—life. Seen from within, the struggle represents the surge of life, and the struggle is dominated by will. It is will in the sense of impulse, life-urge, ecstasy of power, rather than ethical choice. It is presented as an animal trait, inherited and consequently not really "free." If Buck were a man there would have to be some kind of ethical responsibility. With Buck there need be only this animal expression of the life-instinct that is derived from his "racial memory" of his ancestors.

Although the story is seen substantially from Buck's point of view, there is always inevitably present (and carefully controlled by London) the reader's moral judgment of men and their actions. Thus one admires the dogs' noble courage, hates the tenderfeet, and loves the kind John Thornton who saves Buck. Much of the aesthetic effect of the novel attaches to these feelings. Chapter VI is devoted to the love of dog and man, and here the reader's feelings are entirely human and civilized as he responds to the presentation of Buck's devotion to Thornton while in all other respects he is becoming increasingly wild. He twice saves Thornton's life and wins a $1600 wager for him by pulling a tremendous load.

Finally, on a trip into the wilderness, Buck's atavism surges up within him. He has racial dreams of remote times, when fear dominated his primitive master:

> When he watched the hairy man sleeping by the fire, head between his knees and hands clasped above, Buck saw that he slept restlessly, with many starts and awakenings, at which times he would peer fearfully into the darkness and fling more wood upon the fire. . . . Through the forest they crept noiselessly, Buck at the hairy man's heels; and they were alert and vigilant, the pair of them, ears twitching and moving nostrils quivering, for the man heard and smelled as keenly as Buck . . . and Buck had memories of nights of

vigil spent beneath trees wherein the hairy man roosted, holding on tightly as he slept.

The same primordialism that makes him "remember" the hairy man draws him toward the wolves whom he hears howling at night. He makes friends with the pack and, when John Thornton is killed, he joins the pack and lives thereafter as a magnificent wolf—more cunning and fierce than all the others and the relentless foe of the Indians who had killed his master. In this story the conflict of animal impulse and ethical nature is successfully evaded because the hero is a dog of whom ethical action is not expected—though the most moving passages in the book are those that deal with Buck's love for Thornton and which, consequently, appeal strongly to the reader's sense of moral rightness and goodness.

The Call of the Wild is a masterpiece of thrilling and colorful narrative, but it does not—indeed it cannot—tell anything about the nature of "atavism" or the operation of determinism.

The discrepancy between London's philosophical ideas and the "naturalistic" use he is able to make of them in his novels appears in his explanation of *White Fang,* companion volume to *The Call of the Wild.* Published in 1906, *White Fang* deals with a wolf who is domesticated through circumstances and, particularly, the love of a man. London wrote of it:

> Life is full of disgusting realism. I know men and women as they are—millions of them yet in the slime state. But I am an evolutionist, therefore a broad optimist, hence my love for the human (in the slime though he be) comes from my knowing him as he is and seeing the divine possibilities ahead of him. That's the whole motive of my "White Fang." Every atom of organic life is plastic. The finest specimens now in existence were once all pulpy infants capable of being molded this way or that. Let the pressure be one way and we have atavism—the reversion to the wild; the other the domestication, civilization.

As a theory this is all very well, but in the novels there is no explanation of the atavism and the domestication; their only justification is that they *happen.* No "pressures" are depicted which tell why Buck goes wild and White Fang becomes tame. The facts speak for themselves; as facts they are convincing; but the science or philosophy behind them receives no serious attention. It is less real even than Zola's famous "experimental" program.

—Charles Child Walcutt, "Jack London: Blond Beasts and Supermen," *American Literary Naturalism, A Divided Stream* (Minneapolis: University of Minnesota Press, 1956): pp. 105–7.

Earle Labor on the Myth of Hero, Apotheosis, Transformation, and Timelessness

[This excerpt is taken from the article "Jack London's *Mondo Cane: The Call of the Wild* and *White Fang*" by Earle Labor. In the article, Labor concentrates on the myth of the hero.]

Pearl Buck has said that, although great literature does offer escape, it is an escape "deeper into the world and not away from it." *The Call of the Wild* is an "escape" book in this sense. Maxwell Geismar provides an important clue to this deeper meaning when he classifies the work as "a beautiful prose poem, or *nouvelle*, of gold and death on the instinctual level," a "handsome parable of the buried impulses." We need only interpolate that these "buried impulses" are essentially human, not canine, and that the reader identifies with Buck more profoundly than he realizes. Strictly speaking, *The Call* is not a novel but a poem informed by the rhythms of epic and myth. The basic pattern of its action derives from a motif of immemorial antiquity: the Myth of the Hero. The call to adventure, departure, initiation, the perilous journey to the "world navel" or mysterious life-source, transformation, and apotheosis: these are the essential phases of the Myth, and all are present in Buck's progress from the civilized through the natural to the supernatural world. His journey carries him not only through space but also through time and, ultimately, into the still center of a world that is timeless.

Appropriately, London's style accommodates itself to this progress. Aside from the rather clumsy verse epigraph at the beginning of the story, nothing could be more prosaic than the opening sentence: "Buck did not read the newspapers, or he would have known that trouble was brewing, not alone for himself, but for every tidewater dog, strong of muscle and with warm, long hair, from Puget Sound to San Diego." After having been forcibly disabused of his civilized code first by the man in the red sweater, a nicely symbolic figure, and then by his fellow sled-dogs led by Spitz, Buck is now prepared to hear the first faint call of the primeval; and with this change in his character occurs a corresponding stylistic modulation in Chapter 3, "The Dominant Primordial Beast":

> With the aurora borealis flaming coldly overhead, or the stars leaping in the frost dance, and the land numb and frozen under its pall of snow, this song of the huskies might have been the defiance of life, only it was pitched in minor key, with long-drawn wailings and half-sobs, and was more the pleading of life, the articulate travail of existence. It was an old song, old as the breed itself—one of the first songs of the younger world in a day when songs were sad. It was invested with the woe of unnumbered generations, this plaint by which Buck was so strangely stirred. When he moaned and sobbed, it was with the pain of the living that was of old the pain of his wild fathers, and the fear and the mystery of the cold and dark that was to them fear and mystery. And that he should be stirred by it marked the completeness with which he harked back through the ages of fire and roof to the raw beginnings of life in the howling ages.

Moving from prose to poetry and from the material world to the world of myth, London achieves one of his finest passages here, and another near the end of this chapter; both reveal that Buck's is no common animal story:

> There is an ecstasy that marks the summit of life, and beyond which life cannot rise. And such is the paradox of living, this ecstasy comes when one is most alive. This ecstasy, this forgetfulness of living, comes to the artist, caught up and out of himself in a sheet of flame; it comes to the soldier, war-mad on a stricken field and refusing quarter; and it came to Buck, leading the pack, sounding the old wolf-cry, straining after the food that was alive and that fled swiftly before him through the moonlight. He was sounding the deeps of his nature, and of the parts of his nature that were deeper than he, going back into the womb of Time. He was mastered by the sheer surging joy of life, the tidal wave of being, the perfect joy of each separate muscle, joint, and sinew in that it was everything that was not death, that it was aglow and rampant, expressing itself in movement, flying exultantly under the stars and over the face of dead matter that did not move.

This paragraph, a thematic epitome of the whole book, immediately prefaces the weirdly moving scene in which Buck and Spitz engage in fatal battle for leadership of the team, a scene noted by Professor Geismar as "a perfect instance of the 'son-horde' theory which Frazer traced in *The Golden Bough*, and of that primitive ritual to which

Freud himself attributed both a sense of original sin and the fundamental ceremony of religious exorcism."

Even though he has "won to mastership," Buck is still not ready for apotheosis; he is a leader and a hero—but he is not yet divine. His divinity must be confirmed through death and rebirth. Death occurs symbolically—almost literally—in Chapter 5, "The Toil of Trace and Trail," after the hero has suffered through his terrible ordeal under "the newcomers," Hal, Charles, and Mercedes, who are fittingly removed from the scene after they have fulfilled their role in the ritual. Rebirth comes with spring under the protective love of John Thornton, the benign companion who traditionally appears in the Myth to lead the hero toward his goal. Adumbrations of this goal appear in Chapter 6 as Buck grows stronger: "He was older than the days he had seen and the breaths he had drawn. He linked the past with the present, and the eternity behind him throbbed through him in a mighty rhythm to which he swayed as the tides and seasons swayed."

It is in the seventh and final chapter that the hero achieves apotheosis. Here London modulates both setting and style poetically to enhance Buck's transformation. With the sixteen hundred dollars the dog has won miraculously by pulling a sled loaded with a half-ton of flour, Thornton pays off his debts and buys supplies "to journey into the East after a fabled lost mine, the history of which was as old as the history of the country." From the opening paragraph of this chapter it is evident that the place toward which the group is moving is extraordinary: "Many men had sought it; few had found it; and more than a few there were who had never returned from the quest. This lost mine was steeped in tragedy and shrouded in mystery. No one knew of the first man. The oldest tradition stopped before it got back to him." The land into which Thornton's party ventures coincides with that described in *The Hero with a Thousand Faces:*

> [The "call of adventure"] signifies that destiny has summoned the hero and transferred his spiritual center of gravity from within the pale of society to a zone unknown. This fateful region of both treasure and danger may be variously represented: as a distant land, a forest, a kingdom underground, beneath the waves, or above the sky, a secret island, lofty mountaintop, or profound dream state; but it is always a place of strangely fluid and polymorphous beings, unimaginable torments, superhuman deeds and impossible delight.

—Earle Labor, "Jack London's Mondo Cane: *The Call of the Wild and White Fang*," *Jack London Newsletter* 1, no. 1 (July–Dec. 1967): pp. 8–10.

Earl J. Wilcox on the Showdown between Buck and Spitz

[This excerpt comes from Earl J. Wilcox's article "Jack London's Naturalism: The Example of *The Call of the Wild*." In the article, Wilcox discusses the final fight for leadership between Buck and Spitz.]

The lead dog, whose job it is to keep the others in line, even if killing is necessary, is Spitz. From the first, Spitz and Buck have been deadly enemies. When Spitz tries to steal Buck's bed, Buck reacts and "The beast in him roared." Even when Francois or Perrault, the masters, try to separate the dogs, Buck is eager to continue the fracas. Once in the grip of the new morality, ". . . fairplay was a forgotten code" and Buck springs on Spitz. While these minor clashes characterize the long trips which Buck and his friends are making, Buck discovers also that he is soft from years in civilization. Buck's feet tell the tale: ". . . [they] were not so compact and hard as the feet of the huskies. His had softened during the many generations since the day his last wild ancestor was tamed by a cave-dweller or river man."

The inevitable, bloody showdown between Buck and Spitz is soon to come. And "Buck wanted it. He wanted it because it was his nature. . . ." For Buck had endured thus far because he was different from the Southland dogs: "He alone endured and prospered, matching the husky in strength, savagery, and cunning."

London leads his reader along at a rapid pace as he points toward the supreme effort of Buck's life, his fight with Spitz. In the precision of moving toward the battle, London again shows the explicit parallel between the lives of the dogs whom he is describing and the lives of humanity whom he also has in mind. ⟨. . .⟩

Finally, Buck is given the pre-eminent position as leader of the pack because the others respect his strength and his skill. Even Spitz resists open fighting, though grumbling has set in among some of the pack before the final stretch of a long journey between Dawson and Salt Water.

The call which has been haunting Buck returns one evening as he and the others relax after a day in the traces. A snowshoe rabbit is treed and the pack is off after it. While leading the pack in the chase, Buck remembers his primordial past:

> All that stirring of old instincts which at stated periods drives men out from the sounding cities to forest and plain to kill things by chemically propelled leaden pellets, the blood lust, the joy to kill— all this was Buck's, only it was infinitely more intimate. He was ranging at the head of the pack, running the wild thing down, the living meat, to kill with his own teeth and wash his muzzle to the eyes in warm blood.

And in the description of this thrill of the chase, the joy, the ecstasy of living, London evinces a significant materialistic attitude that links him profoundly with the naturalists. Buck becomes, perhaps, the epitome of London's own materialistic impulses, in his exulting in the joy of living, the joy of life for its own sake. For Buck is also "mastered by the verb 'to live,'" in precisely the same manner of Jan, the Unrepentant, and Sturgis Owens, and Scruff Mackenzie—all human protagonists in London's first short stories. Later, London depicted Wolf Larsen, a man, in similar terms; here it is Buck, the dog, who finds the life-urge, the sense of impulse, the will to live, dominating all else.

> —Earl J. Wilcox, "Jack London's Naturalism: The Example of *The Call of the Wild*," *Jack London Newsletter* 2, no. 3 (Sept.–Dec. 1969): pp. 96–97.

᠗

MARY KAY DODSON ON HEREDITY, BIOLOGY, AND THE ENVIRONMENT IN THE STORY

[This excerpt is from the article "Naturalism in the Works of Jack London" by Mary Kay Dodson. Dodson here discusses the place of heredity in *The Call of the Wild* and the influence of the environment.]

In *The Call of the Wild*, the portrayal of men as beasts is shown as well as the portrayal of dog as beast. When Buck is caged after he has been stolen, he is tormented by his captors. He has been put in a baggage car and has had nothing to eat or drink for two days. As can be expected, Buck is very angry. "In his anger he had met the first advances of the express messengers with growls, and they had retaliated by teasing him. When he flung himself against the bars, quivering and frothing, they laughed at him and taunted him. They growled and barked like detestable dogs. . . ."

Buck's first introduction to primitive law—the law of the club and fang—came at the hands of Perrault who beat him into submission with a club. Buck learned quickly that he must avoid the club; he was an intelligent dog who fought not only by instinct, but also by his head. He "possessed a quality that made for greatness—imagination." His imagination helped him not only to survive, but also to adapt.

Buck's father was a huge St. Bernard and his mother a Scotch shepherd dog. During the four years he lived at Judge Miller's, he became accustomed to the genteel life. "But he had saved himself by not becoming a mere pampered house dog. Hunting and kindred outdoor delights had kept down the fat and hardened his muscles; and to him, as to the cold-tubbing races, the love of water had been a tonic and a health preserver." Because Buck was in good physical condition, one aspect of his adaptation to the Yukon territory was made easier; he was capable of doing the work for which he had been stolen.

The powerful influence of Buck's heredity is carefully presented. He was not homesick because his memories of California were very dim and distant, and therefore not very powerful. "For more potent were the memories of his heredity that gave things he had never seen before a seeming familiarity; the instincts (which were but the memories of his ancestors become habits) which had lapsed in later days, and still later, in him, quickened and became alive again." Even though Buck's father too had been a companion of Judge Miller's, Buck quickly recognized his hereditary instincts. He responded to them because he was placed in an environment in which these hereditary factors were essential to survival. Had he remained in his comfortable surroundings at the ranch, he never would have felt this influence of his heredity.

Buck realized that his new environment was his natural habitat especially when he made friends with the wolf. The two of them

came down into a level country where were great stretches of forest and many streams, and through these great stretches they ran steadily, hour after hour, the sun rising higher and the day growing warmer. Buck was wildly glad. He knew he was at last answering the call, running by the side of his wood brother toward the place from where the call surely came. Old memories were coming upon him fast, and he was stirring to them as of old he stirred to the realities of which they were the shadows. He had done this thing before, somewhere in that other and dimly remembered world, and he was doing it again, now, running free in the open, the unpacked earth underfoot, the wide sky overhead.

Buck, in responding to the call of the wild, was responding to the call of his ancestors—his heredity. As his hereditary forces came into the fore, he began to depend less and less upon the only decent human being he had encountered since leaving Judge Miller's. He learned to kill, but not just for the sake of killing; he killed to feed himself. "The blood longing became stronger than ever before. He was a killer, a thing that preyed, living on the things that lived, unaided, alone, by virtue of his own strength and prowess, surviving triumphantly in a hostile environment when only the strong survived. Because of all this he became possessed of a great pride in himself, which communicated itself like a contagion to his physical being." His appearance was almost that of a gigantic wolf. The physical characteristics of his father and mother were blended in him:

From his St. Bernard father he had inherited size and weight, but it was his shepherd mother who had given shape to that size and weight. His muzzle was the long wolf muzzle, save that it was larger than the muzzle of any wolf; and his head, somewhat broader, was the wolf head on a massive scale. His cunning was wolf cunning, and wild cunning; his intelligence, shepherd intelligence and St. Bernard intelligence; and all this, plus an experience gained in the fiercest of schools, made him as formidable a creature as any that roamed the wild.

Thus Buck explicitly embodies the theory of naturalism. He is a product of biological, environmental, and hereditary forces.

—Mary Kay Dodson, "Naturalism in the Works of Jack London," *Jack London Newsletter* 4, no. 3 (Sept.–Dec. 1971): pp. 132–34.

[This excerpt is taken from Charles N. Watson's book *The Novels of Jack London: A Reappraisal,* from the chapter entitled "Ghost Dog: *The Call of the Wild.*" In the chapter, Watson compares *The Call of the Wild* with *Huckleberry Finn,* concluding that the novels are very similar.]

This indigenous American quality can be seen more clearly if one observes the structural parallels between *The Call of the Wild* and *Adventures of Huckleberry Finn.* As the two novels begin, each young protagonist lives in society under the protection of a benevolent foster parent. Each undertakes a journey away from that sheltered world, encountering in his travels several varieties of civilized virtue and folly. Intermittently, however, he feels the counterinfluence of the natural world and the anarchic impulse toward escape; and when each at the end is nearly adopted by another benevolent foster parent, he instead heeds the call of the wild and lights out for the Territory.

Despite manifest differences of tone and narrative method—*The Call,* for example, lacks the satirical, picaresque qualities of Twain's novel—these structural and thematic parallels suggest that both *Huckleberry Finn* and *The Call* are sustained at least in part by a common vision. What they share is the perennial American dream of escape and freedom associated with the natural world. As critics of *Huckleberry Finn* have repeatedly recognized, it is the river itself, and the life Huck and Jim lead there, that holds the strongest fascination for the reader. In this idyllic world, the stirrings of primitive life reassert themselves when the two fugitives, rejecting the dessicated piety of civilization, reinvent a natural mythology as they speculate about the origin of the stars, wondering "whether they was made, or only just happened." Jim suggests that "the moon could a *laid* them," and Huck allows that "that looked kind of reasonable . . . because I've seen a frog lay most as many, so of course it could be done." Just as Huck begins to reexperience the world mythopoetically, from the ground up and from the sky down, London's Buck must discover, in himself and in the wilderness, the primordial sensations that lead him to reject the conventions of civilized life. Hence it is no disparagement to say that both of these are "escape novels," for the impulse toward escape—toward the world of wish and dream—exists in all of us, and one of the functions of fiction is to fulfill it. There is, no doubt, a higher function that fiction can serve: to take us not merely away from our daily realities but into a reality we have not yet experienced or have experienced only imperfectly. The best "escape fiction"—including *Huckleberry Finn* and *The Call of the Wild*—serves that purpose, too.

During the long middle section of the novel, Buck is at the mercy of his owners, and the structure of episodes is governed chiefly by the contrast between two Klondike types, the hardened sourdough and the ignorant *chechaquo*. Francois and Perrault, with their rough but humane discipline and their hardy devotion to work, contrast sharply with the hapless incapables: the mindlessly vicious Hal and Charles, who club the dogs for failing to perform impossible tasks, and the self-indulgent, sentimental Mercedes, who protests the whipping of the "poor dears" even while insisting that the bone-weary dogs pull her own weight on the already overloaded sled. This trio, in turn, contrasts sharply with Buck's final master, the kindly John Thornton.

But these episodes offer more than a gallery of Klondike types. They also serve to establish the civilized values against which the wilderness must compete, for human society in this novel is not an irredeemable disaster. Indeed, its most attractive virtues serve as a necessary counterweight to the ever more insistent call of the wild. Of central though qualified value is the pride of work, and even more deeply attractive is the value of love. For Buck, both love and work fulfill a profound need, though neither can finally compete with the deepest need of all—the one ecstatically fulfilled in the blood ritual of the hunt.

—Charles N. Watson Jr., "Ghost Dog: *The Call of the Wild*," *The Novels of Jack London: A Reappraisal* (Madison: University of Wisconsin Press, 1983): pp. 39–41.

Plot Summary of
"The She-Wolf"

"The She-Wolf" is part of *White Fang*, a novel London meant to be a companion to *The Call of the Wild*. Whereas *The Call* told the story of a dog becoming wild, *White Fang* told the story of a wolf becoming tame. It was never as great a success as *The Call*, much to London's disappointment.

"The She-Wolf" is the story of Bill and Henry, two trappers who are transporting the body of Lord Alfred, an Englishman who died in the wild. They are taking the body back to civilization so it can be shipped home for burial.

One night, when Bill feeds the sled dogs, he discovers seven dogs eating instead of the expected six . The next morning, he finds only five dogs. The men know they are being followed by a pack of hungry wolves, but as their dogs continue to disappear one by one, the men cannot understand why the dogs are leaving the camp, only to be eaten; their dogs should have more sense than that. Henry and Bill realize that a wolf must have come into the camp to be fed along with the dogs, but why, the men wonder, didn't the dogs react to the wolf?

When another dog, Frog, goes missing, the men tie up the dogs at night with sticks around their necks so they can't chew off their bindings. The dog Anchor, however, is chewed loose by another dog; all the men find of him is his stick. Bill and Henry grow increasingly uneasy, especially since they have only three cartridges left for their guns.

The mystery of their dogs' behavior is solved when the men discover that a she-wolf has been luring the male dogs away from camp to be killed. She is clearly not afraid of people, and when they try to shoot her, she gets away, leading them to suspect that she is familiar with guns.

Meanwhile, the starving wolves are getting bolder as they follow the two men and their dogs. Henry and Bill are forced to wake up in the night to scare the pack away from their camp. Bill is depressed, and as the story closes, Henry resolves to cheer him up. The future for the two men, however, looks dark and foreboding. ❀

List of Characters in
"The She-Wolf"

Bill and Henry are two trappers transporting the body of another man.

Lord Alfred is the dead Englishman whose body is being carried back to civilization. Such an act was unusual and indicates Lord Alfred's wealth and importance.

The She-Wolf is a female wolf with an unusual reddish color that allows her to blend in with Bill and Henry's huskies. She lures the dogs away, and her pack kills them for food.

Frog is one of the dogs who goes missing.

Anchor is a dog who is chewed loose from his bindings by another dog, only to be eaten by the wolves. ❀

Critical Views on
"The She-Wolf"

MAXWELL GEISMAR ON THE DEATH IMPULSE IN
WHITE FANG

[This excerpt is from the chapter "Jack London: The Short
Cut: That Long Heart-Broken Puppy Wail," from Maxwell
Geismar's book *Rebels and Ancestors: The American Novel,
1890–1915*. Here, Geismar expounds on the place of the
death impulse in *White Fang*.]

⟨*White Fang*⟩ was concerned quite literally with the death impulses
which apparently, in London's case as in Freud's, were dominant in
nature itself—or at least were primary in the key episodes and
prevailing imagery of London's second animal fable.

There was a deliberate parallel with the bull moose who was
tracked down by the "clinging terror" of the wolves in the earlier
story.

> The big bull was beset on every side. . . . He crushed them and broke
> them on his large horns. He stamped them into the snow under him
> in the wallowing struggle. But he was foredoomed, and he went down
> with the she-wolf tearing savagely at his throat, and with other teeth
> fixed everywhere upon him, devouring him alive before ever his last
> struggles ceased. . . .

But here of course the stress was on brutal destruction, and the
"wallowing struggle" of blood and flesh. The introduction to
primitive love, with its recurrent undertones of the Freudian son-
horde when the young wolves grouped together to destroy the
leader and gain possession of the she-wolf, was even "a sterner and
crueler business than that of food-getting." When the she-wolf has
her litter, she protects it also against her own mate, for "there
lurked a memory of fathers that had eaten their new-born and
helpless progeny."

That was the birth of White Fang, and the savagery of animal
relationships was treated brilliantly in the story. Or of relationships
on the animal level, and the reduction of all love, affection or sense
of trust and guardianship to an oral context, stronger, more

continuous and basic than the sexual drive itself. The law of life became only and purely the law of meat in another key episode where the old wolf and the female lynx both lay in wait for a porcupine to open himself up. "The waiting lynx and the waiting porcupine, each intent on life; and such was the curiousness of the game, the way of life for one lay in the eating of the other, and the way of life for the other lay in being not eaten." When the porcupine exposed himself at last, and the lynx had ripped open his stomach, which was still "trying feebly to roll up into its ball-protection" in spite of its disrupted anatomy, the wolf, as spectator of this savage drama, felt only an involuntary desire for "the living meat that was spreading itself like a repast before him." These pages of *White Fang* are indeed a parable of horrors, a lyric poem of barbarism in which all the dark aspects of organic life had become concentrated in the drooling of the gastric juices.

The quality of this little epic of brute survival was of course highly symbolistic—as in the episode of the rabbit that had been fastened to a bent tree, and that, when the tree was released, danced wildly in the air above the terrified wolves. (The rabbit whose head was gnawed off by the she-wolf who understood the workings of the Indian snare.) If London was showing the double force in nature—to increase life and to limit it—the destructive impulses and that eloquent "cessation of movement" were dominant here. And food itself, staff of these gruesome origins of existence, almost seemed in the end to be only the nourishment of corpses, or the high-flavored delicacies of death. . . . The impartial tone was maintained throughout. The chronicle of horrors was related with a certain tenderness, even, for the tortured barbarisms of natural existence. The structure of the story moved back from the world of men—"the animal that had fought itself to primacy" but the least attractive animal to London's eyes—to the world of animals. It is interesting to notice the cruel-tender tone in London's descriptions of the wolf-cub's early battles with the ptarmigan chicks and the hawk (here the blood-lust became completely lyrical), or in the encounter with the weasel's "lean, snakelike body, and her head, erect, eager, and snakelike itself." Here, too, were almost the only true moments of emotion on a nongustatory level, when the mother wolf nuzzled and caressed her cub in a brief "access of affection"; or of the tragic mood itself in that "long heart-broken puppy wail" when White Fang was abandoned by her and converted to the law of 'civilization.'

He learns to "oppress the weak and obey the strong" and becomes in turn the enemy of his kind.

The cry of a brokenhearted youth—of an outcast in a world of horrors—is a familiar refrain in London's work. It was illuminating that the last memorable episode in the wolf-dog's apprenticeship should be that of the bulldog's grip on his throat. ("It made him frantic, this clinging, dragging weight. . . . It was like a trap.") While the bulldog's stumpy tail, in the blind horrors of nature and civilization alike, continued to wag vigorously. . . . The Clinging Death indeed! It was only when White Fang was rescued from these extremes of cruelty and terror, to become "the blessed wolf" of a gracious California estate in the Southland, a perfect pet of an aristocratic gentry, that London succumbed to the sentiment which spoiled another beautiful little parable of the instinctual life.

—Maxwell Geismar, "Jack London: The Short Cut: That Long Heart-Broken Puppy Wail," *Rebels and Ancestors: The American Novel, 1890–1915* (Cambridge: Riverside Press, 1953): pp. 181–83.

⊗

EARL J. WILCOX ON WHITE FANG'S WORLD

[This excerpt is from Earl J. Wilcox's article "*Le Milieu, Le Moment, La Race*: Literary Naturalism in Jack London's *White Fang*." In the article, Wilcox describes the type of world into which White Fang is born.]

Part I of the novel, primarily description of setting, ends with the hungry wolf-pack almost killing the men. For in a series of tensely described episodes the men fight off a pack of wolves which devours the trappers' dogs one by one, and which wait patiently until, the men defeated by the hostile environment, they will devour them also. Bill's foolish attempt to kill the pack with his meagre supply of ammunition leads to his death, but Charlie survives the nightmare. These opening episodes are grotesquely presented, in a way, for men do not belong in the land of the White Silence, London implies. It is a bleak, desolate, and merciless world. Yet, it is but one aspect of universal experience. For, while ostensibly this is just a world where wolves and their brothers live and where nature works her woe on all trespassers, London soon makes clear how precisely the forests are but another setting of the same pitiless universe in which man constantly lives. In speaking later of Fang as a cub, London notes the parallel:

> Had the cub thought in man-fashion, he might have epitomized life as a voracious appetite, and the world as a place wherein ranged a multitude of appetites, pursuing and being pursued, hunting and being hunted, eating and being eaten, all in blindness and confusion, with violence and disorder, a chaos of gluttony and slaughter, ruled over by chance, merciless, planless, endless.

But being a cub, Fang is born into the world of the big moose, where an ambitious three-year-old suitor of Fang's mother meets exactly the same fate as Curly in *The Call of the Wild*. Buck had learned his first lesson in survival tactics in Curly's death. The description here in the later novel is a parallel enactment of that scene, the death of the suitor being at "the merciless fangs of his erstwhile comrades." And during the love-making season before Fang is conceived, too, the she-wolf is characterized in a familiar materialistic, sensuous role of living for momentary pleasure. The battle for her pleasure is but another "law" of survival in the Wild, and its victors, like Buck, find the summit of living gratifying:

> She was made glad in vague ways by the battle, for this was the love-making of the Wild, the sex-tragedy of the natural world that was tragedy only to those that died. To those that survived it was not tragedy, but realization and achievement.

The eventual victor is One-Eye, Fang's father, with whom the she-wolf makes a home.

Within a brief time cubs are born, and London is offered brief opportunity in the novel for telling of One-Eye's "memories" which, in substance, closely resemble Buck's "visions" in his retrogression to the Wild. Hearing the cubs whining, One-Eye recalls that the sounds are "remotely familiar." And the mother herself has the same "atavistic and barbaric" nature which prompts her also to have vague premonitions. The point of all this is that if meaningful in larger context London's naturalistic creations have vague, undefined feelings about a primordial state. The culmination of the parallels between the man and animal world is in *Before Adam*.

But the memories fade, and One-Eye must provide food for the family. And in the animal's journeys in quest of food London observes once more, as he has averred earlier through Fortune la Perle and numerous others, that life is unpredictable and a gamble, or, in Darwinian terms, the result of a series of accidents. One-Eye stalks a porcupine reciting the lines London readers have come by now to expect:

> But he had long since learned that there was such a thing as Chance, or Opportunity, and he continued to draw near. There was never any telling what might happen, for with live things events were somehow always happening differently.

Perhaps the most thorough analysis of the survival of the fittest and natural selection thesis in London's fiction is given in an episode later in the same day. In hope of getting prime food for the family meal, One-Eye catches first a ptarmigan, then waits for hours for better game, the lynx. The objective manner in which London views the scene might easily be that of a zoologist watching the entire incident in a glass cage:

> He lay down in the snow, depositing the ptarmigan beside him, and with eyes peering through the needles of a low-growing spruce he watched the play of life before him—the waiting lynx and the waiting porcupine, each intent on life; and such was the curiousness of the game, the way of life for one lay in the eating of the other, and the way of life for the other lay in being not eaten. While old One-Eye, the wolf, crouching in the covert, played his part, too, in the game, waiting for some strange freak of Chance, that might help him on the meat-trail which was his way of life.

The horrors and the battle to death struggles are observed with the keen eye of a reporter and analyst. The tone never falters in its massive swiftness and in its brutality. London indicates that he is at home in describing the environment of Fang's world. Indeed the style throughout the description of the wolf-lynx-porcupine struggle is Hemingwayish in its clipped, austere sentence structure, particularly in the details of One-Eye's attempt to provoke the porcupine to life after it has been mauled by the lynx:

> With a nervous, shrinking paw, One-Eye stretched out the porcupine to its full length and turned it over on its back. Nothing happened. It was surely dead. He studied it intently for a moment, then took a careful grip with his teeth and started off down the stream. . . . He

recollected something, dropped the burden, and trotted back to where he had left the ptarmigan. He did not hesitate a moment. He knew clearly what was to be done. . . .

Almost half way through the novel London finally introduces his central character. The "milieu" has been detailed, the "moment" is right, and as representative of his "race," Fang enters the world. And it is a world dominated by creatures of instinct who recognize that happiness is momentary, and in their recognition the inhabitants frequently voice a pessimistic attitude because of the lack of something more permanent. Yet, paradoxically, their materialism also spurs the citizens to live life to its fullest capacity. To be sure, this is London's world, thinly disguised in the study of a wolf's progression to a dog.

> —Earl J. Wilcox, "*Le Milieu, Le Moment, La Race*: Literary Naturalism in Jack London's *White Fang*," *Jack London Newsletter* 3, no. 2 (May–Aug. 1970): pp. 45–48.

⊗

Lynn DeVore on the Biblical Aspects of *White Fang*

[This excerpt comes from DeVore's article "The Descent of White Fang." She discusses some biblical elements in the novel.]

White Fang's journey of descent is particularly evidenced through the novel's own structure and through the use of a Biblical theme. The general framework is like that of a play consisting of five distinct parts nicely balanced, a clean, classic design: After the marvelous opening prologue about two men fighting for survival in the bleak Northland wilds (one of the best short stories London ever wrote), the remaining sections are each divided into five or six interchapters—parts two and five have five chapters, parts three and four have six. Occasionally London is able to exploit this pattern by juxtaposing subject in parallel sections. At the center, for example, the sixth chapter of both parts three and four fall alongside one another in the total geometric design. They are entitled "Famine" and "The Love Master"; the obvious opposition of physical opposition to spiritual supplement is to be noted. London does not, though, balance all parts of his interchapters perfectly and symmetrically. Such exacting precision would appear too contrived. Instead, it seems he chose to subtly weave a Biblical theme through the tidy arrangement, a theme which heavily aids his structure, but one which, ironically, will buttress White Fang's downward journey.

White Fang begins his life in a totally natural world, the wilderness untrammelled by civilization. As a young cub he learns fear, defense, the thrill of killing for survival. London is careful to relate that the hero learns a primitive natural law: "The aid of life was meat. Life itself was meat. Life lived on life. There were the eaters and the eaten. The law was: EAT OR BE EATEN. He did not formulate the law in clear, set terms and moralize about it. He did not even think the law; he merely lived the law without thinking about it at all."

When White Fang meets the Makers of Fire, the first taste of civilization, he is forced to learn a new code. Within this world, moreover, he learns quickly and emerges as a kind of Nietzschean superdog—he is superior. In the "Outcast" chapter we are told, ". . . his development was rapid and one-sided. This was no soil for kindness and affection to blossom in. . . . The code he learned was to obey the strong and to oppress the weak. . . . His development was in the direction of power."

It is important that the new code which he acquires appears in the chapter entitled "The Covenant," for it recalls, or alludes to, the Old Testament covenant made between God and man when an eye for an eye, tooth for a tooth (fang for fang if you will) was the law. Like Job, White Fang too must obey his master however harsh the treatment; then he will be rewarded. White Fang's first faithful act toward man, which involves the law of property, occurs when he attacks some boys when stealing meat; in return he is greatly rewarded. London also distinguishes the new code from any which might involve love: "White Fang's was a service of duty and awe, but not of love. He did not know what love was. He had no experience of love. Kiche was a remote memory. Besides, not only had he abandoned the wild and his kind when he gave himself up to man, but the terms of the covenant were such that if he ever met Kiche again he would not desert his god to go with her. His allegiance to man seemed somehow a law of his being greater than the love of liberty, of kind and kin." This is the law of the Old Testament, the law of discipline and obedience.

At this point in the narrative White Fang falls into the hands of the satanic Beauty Smith under whose tutelage the law of hate is learned. We can speculate, moreover, that he has fallen into the state of sin from which the old covenant could not save him. He is the enemy of himself as well as his own kind until he greets the clinging death of the bulldog's jaws. This brief touch with death is, of course, meant to symbolize the end of the Old Testament Man, the demise of the Old Pauline Man. He is then regenerated through love, and Weedon Scott functions in the role of Christ as redeemer: "Weedon Scott had set himself the task of redeeming White Fang—or rather, of redeeming mankind from the wrong it had done White Fang. It was a matter of principle and conscience. He felt that the ill done White Fang was a debt incurred by man and that it must be paid." The New Testament allusions are all too obvious.

Ironically, it is the adoption of this new social code which weakens White Fang forcing him into a "slave morality." No Nietzschean individualist would clothe himself in the garb of the unfit. Selfishness, cunning, amorality—these bring happiness to the individual through the indulgence of a will to power. Nietzsche, himself, consistently taught that all ethical ideas which teach self denial or restraint are evil doctrines designed to protect the weak. This code of love is a false truth. London's description of White Fang's new life is devastating: "It was the beginning of the end for White Fang—the ending of the old life and the reign of hate. A new and incomprehensibly fairer life was dawning. It required much thinking and endless patience on the part of Weedon Scott to accomplish this. And on the part of White Fang it required nothing less than a revolution. He had to ignore the urges and promptings of instinct and reason, defy experience, give the lie to life itself."

But White Fang's regeneration is ironic—from this juncture the book assumes a downward course. This pattern is not new to London's fiction either. Gordon Mill's interesting essay, "Jack London's Quest for Salvation," traces the love theme through most of the novels. His conclusion is the same: "In every instance this love theme symbolized an attack upon unrestrained individualism and brutality."

—Lynn DeVore, "The Descent of White Fang," *Jack London Newsletter* 7, no. 3 (Sept.–Dec. 1974): pp. 123–24.

DONALD PIZER ON *WHITE FANG* COMPARED TO *THE CALL OF THE WILD*

[This excerpt is taken from the chapter "Jack London: The Problem of Form" from Donald Pizer's book *Realism and Naturalism in Nineteenth-Century American Literature.* In the chapter, Pizer compares London's two dog novels, *White Fang* and *The Call of the Wild.*]

The Call of the Wild and *White Fang* are companion allegories of the response of human nature to heredity and environment. Both Buck and White Fang begin their lives with a mixture of the primitive and the civilized in their condition. Buck is raised in the Southland (London's allegorical setting for civilization), but, like all dogs, has an atavistic strain of wolf in his make-up. White Fang, though largely wolf and though bred in the Far North, contains an element of the civilized through his part-dog mother. The novels demonstrate the effects of a change in environment on the two dogs. Buck, abducted into a Northland world of the ruthless struggle for existence, calls forth from his racial past the strength and cunning necessary to survive in this world, and eventually becomes the leader of a wolf-pack in a people-less wilderness. White Fang is drawn into civilization, first by Indians, then by miners, and finally, in the Southland, by upper middle class ranchers, and becomes doglike in his loyalty and love toward his master.

What appeals in the two works is not London's dramatization of a particular late nineteenth-century Darwinian formulation but rather his powerful use of the principal ethical thrust and formal characteristics of the fable, with an admixture as well of the parable. Characterization is at a minimum in the two works; dogs and men are types and the types themselves are moral in nature. In *Call*, Charles, Hal, and Mercedes (the three "tenderfoot" Klondikers who buy Buck) are Vanity and Ignorance, and John Thornton is Loyalty and Love. The dogs in the story are even more clearly moral types—

Laziness, Envy, Fear, Honesty, and so on. In *White Fang*, Kiche is the Mother, Beauty Smith (who exhibits White Fang) is Evil, and Weedon Scott is Thornton's counterpart. Setting is allegorical in both works, with London exaggerating for symbolic clarity both the "softness" of the South and the competitive animality of the North. And action is symbolic within the clear lines of thematic movement of Buck's return to the primitive and White Fang's engagement by civilization. Perhaps most important of all, theme itself is essentially proverbial rather than ideological. It is not so much Darwin and Spencer who supply the thematic core of the two novels as Aesop and the Bible. For *Call of the Wild* proposes the wisdom of the beast fable that the strong, the shrewd, and the cunning shall prevail when, as is progressively true in this story, life is bestial. And *White Fang* endorses the Christian wisdom that all shall lie down together in peace when love predominates.

Both *Call* and *White Fang* contain—to a degree not usually sufficiently stressed—a strong element of the Christian parable within their beast fable emphasis on the competitive nature of experience. Buck's response to the kindness, justness, and warmth of Thornton is love; it is only with the death of Thornton that he becomes the Ghost Dog of the wilderness. And White Fang, when rescued from the brutality of Beauty Smith by Weedon Scott and when "educated" in affection by Scott, also responds with love. The moral allegory is clear in both works. Man hovers between the primitive and the civilized both in his make-up and in his world, and it is his capacity for love which often determines which direction he will take. Again, this theme is not so much specifically ideological as it is racial wisdom, with that wisdom embodied in a form which makes it pleasingly evident.

—Donald Pizer, "Jack London: The Problem of Form," *Realism and Naturalism in Nineteenth-Century American Literature*, rev. ed. (Carbondale: Southern Illinois University Press, 1984): pp. 170–72.

James Lundquist on the Overarching Idea of *White Fang*

[This excerpt comes from James Lundquist's book *Jack London: Adventures, Ideas, and Fiction,* from the chapter "Meditations on Man and Beast." Here, Lundquist elaborates on what he sees as the main idea in *White Fang.*]

White Fang was published after London's marriage to Charmian, and it reflects London's own decision to tame his appetites, if he could. The reviews were good, and London was properly praised for the novel's greatest strength: its animal side. "Mr. London has fortunately obeyed the call of the wild and returned to the field of his early triumphs," intoned *The Independent.* "This is quite a relief after the mediocre short stories he has been giving us of late. He apparently understands the psychology of brutes, animal and human better than ordinary tamed and civilized men and women." *The Nation* was more succinct: "As a biographer of wild animals he has hardly an equal."

Like *A Daughter of the Snows,* however, *White Fang* is too deliberately a novel of ideas. The story is structured like an experiment. It is as if London asked himself what would happen if an animal three-quarters wolf and one-quarter dog were suddenly shifted from one environment to another. What does happen is essentially believable, but it is not a very good story. How much more satisfying is the final image of Buck running at the head of the wolf pack than is the final cute picture of White Fang and his puppies. But the main problem is the relentless thesis.

Even though Jim Hall is bent on murdering Judge Scott in his bed, London emphasizes that Hall is not to be blamed for his intention. Hall was "ill-made in the making," London tells us; though Hall is "so terrible a beast that he can best be characterized as carnivorous," it is not his fault. "The more fiercely he fought, the more harshly society handled him, and the only effect of harshness was to make him fiercer," London lectures. "Straight-jackets, starvation, and beatings and clubbings were the wrong treatment for Jim Hall; but it was the treatment he received. It was the treatment he had received from the time he was a little pulpy boy in a San Francisco slum— soft clay in the hands of society and ready to be formed into something." As if this is not enough, we are also told that Hall indeed was wrongfully sent to prison, that the Judge was unwittingly "party to a police conspiracy, that the evidence was hatched and perjured, that Jim Hall was guiltless of the crime charged." Such things can happen, but it is best not to have them happen in fiction. The review that appeared in *The Forum* was, appropriately enough, a slashing one: "It would be an exaggeration to call this novel a Socialistic tract in disguise, but it is not the least clever stroke of its author's that he has succeeded in interweaving into a dog and wolf story so subtle a reminder of the pressure of feral conditions in the midst of civilized human society."

—James Lundquist, "Meditations on Man and Beast," *Jack London: Adventures, Ideas, and Fiction* (New York: Ungar, 1987): pp. 111–12.

Plot Summary of
"The Apostate"

London drew on his own experiences in the jute mill to write this story. It was eventually instrumental in changing the child labor laws.

"The Apostate" tells the story of Johnny, a boy who has worked in the factories almost his whole life. He is 12 years old at the beginning of the story, and he works in the same jute mill his mother was working in when she gave birth to him on the floor. He has never known anything but the sound of machinery.

Although he has a number of younger brothers and sisters, they do not work in the mill. This seems unfair to Johnny; he feels that ten-year-old Will, the next oldest, should at least be starting work. His mother insists that Will is too young, even though he is quite a bit older than Johnny was when he started.

Johnny's life is a tedious one. Each morning, before dawn, his mother drags him out of bed, then forces him to wash before they eat breakfast. Breakfast consists of bread and a muddy liquid that Johnny thinks of as excellent coffee; occasionally, he eats a small piece of cold meat as well. After the long workday, he has his supper and then goes to bed, only to repeat the pattern the next day.

Johnny remembers a time when life was not so tedious, but he doesn't remember actually being allowed to play and be a child. From a very early age he had to look after Will and the others. When he was seven, he went to work at the jute mill, winding bobbins, and the next year, he worked at a cloth mill. This was an easy job, and he was still young enough to be able to imagine and dream while he worked. He lost this job, however, when he got the measles. After this, he worked in a glass factory, doing piecework; his job there was to tie glass stoppers into small bottles. He was very good at it: he could tie 300 dozen bottles a day. He lost this job, however, when he got pneumonia from the hunched-over position in which he had to work. Now he is back at the jute mill where he started.

There are several great events in his life that he remembers: when his mother bought prunes, when she made custard, and when he found a quarter. He also vaguely recalls his father as a savage thing, but usually that memory comes to him only as he is falling asleep.

As time moves on, Johnny is promoted first to the loom in the jute mill, and then, when he is 14, to the starcher. This promotion is a huge event in Johnny's life, and he marks time by it, dividing his life into before and after the starcher. When he is 16, though, he goes back to the loom, where it is piecework and he can make more money. He is becoming a perfect machine; finally he can even work four looms at the same time.

By now, he is making more money, but the more he makes, the more he seems to need; the children are eating more as they grow up, and since they are in school, there are schoolbooks to be bought.

When he is 17 or 18, he falls ill with "la grippe." He is in bed for a week and then given another week by the doctor to recover. While Johnny is recovering, he sits on the front step staring at the tree across the road. He asks his brother to show him how to do calculations, and for a long time he sits with a paper and pencil, doing arithmetic. After he finishes the calculations, he simply sits, staring at the tree.

At the beginning of the third week, his mother urges him to get up and go to work. Since he is such a good worker, his job has been saved for him, but Johnny refuses to get up. He just wants to go back to sleep. Frightened by what she considers his insanity, his mother calls the doctor, who says there is nothing wrong with him.

Johnny gets up several hours later and goes downstairs to tell his mother—who has not gone to work either—that he is going away and that he just wanted to say good-bye. She is shocked and appalled. He is tired out, he says—he's tired of moving. He has calculated that when he was younger he made about 12 million moves a year at the factories, and now, on the looms, he makes about 25 million moves a year. The sheer amount of movements he has been making all his life has worn him out.

When his mother wonders, sobbing, what will happen to Will and the other children, Johnny says that Will can go to work. Their mother has been hoping that Will will finish school and become a bookkeeper. Although Johnny speaks with no bitterness or anger, his life is clearly unfair; Will is larger and heavier because he has never had to work, while Johnny is smaller because he was undernourished and overworked.

Johnny leaves, walking slowly toward the railway station. His figure as he walks does not look like a man's; he is twisted and stunted and grotesque. All afternoon, he lies in the grass by the railway station, sleeping or watching the birds and sky. When the sky grows dark, he climbs into an empty boxcar, lies down, and smiles. ❁

List of Characters in
"The Apostate"

Johnny is a boy wizened and deformed by constant labor in the mills and factories from the time he was seven years old. He becomes an adolescent at age seven when he starts work, and a man at age eleven when he works the night shift. He measures his life by the machines he has worked, and he is almost a machine himself. When he is 18 or so, he gets sick, and after he recovers, he decides he has worked too much in life. He leaves home, planning to never work again.

Johnny's mother is a sad and tired woman. Although she and her oldest son work in the mills, she wants to protect her younger children from this lifestyle, hoping to put them through school to give them a better life. She knows she has mistreated Johnny, but she doesn't know what else she could have done.

Will is Johnny's brother. He is two years younger than Johnny but goes to school instead of working at the mills. He is larger and heavier than Johnny. He may have to drop out of school to begin work when Johnny leaves. ❀

Critical Views on
"The Apostate"

FRANKLIN WALKER ON LONDON'S MARXIST FICTION

[This excerpt is from an article by Franklin Walker, "Ideas and Action in Jack London's Fiction," published in the book *Essays on American Literature in Honor of Jay B. Hubbell*, edited by Clarence Gohdes. In the article, Walker talks about London's socialist fiction in general, as well as *The Iron Heel* in particular.]

With the exception of one or two short stories like ⟨"The Apostate" and⟩ "The Mexican" and a handful of essays, *The Iron Heel* is the only work by London to reflect in any detail his enthusiasm for socialism and particularly Marxism. During the year before its composition he had lectured widely throughout the United States in support of the Intercollegiate Socialist Society, of which he was the first president; often sounding more revolutionary than his supporters, he had come to feel, in the face of the proletarian revolts in the Russia of 1905, that violence rather than the ballot was the true path for the socialist in America. His picture of the social and economic struggle in *The Iron Heel*, written in 1906 and published shortly after the staggering shock of the panic of 1907, emphasized the weakness of socialist reform achieved through parliamentary procedures and pictured the rise of totalitarianism imposed by big business which by 1918 would crush the working class under "the iron heel of a despotism as relentless and terrible as any despotism that has blackened the pages of the history of man." Though the novel forecasts an eventual victory for the proletariat in three hundred years, it does so only through footnotes; its action ends in a most fearful blood bath when the proletarian revolutionists, who have been driven underground, set up a short-lived commune in Chicago. Though *The Iron Heel* impressed such widely different rebels as Eugene Debs, Anatole France, and Leon Trotsky, and though it has received considerable credit for anticipating fascism, its significance as an exposition of Marxist ideology is not today taken very seriously. According to Deming Brown in his *Soviet Attitudes toward American Writing*, more than thirty years ago the Russian critics decided that the novel showed a very faulty conception of Marxism and it is today read in Russia principally as a picture of contemporary American society! The Russians, who have published more works by London than by any other American writer, are fascinated by his books about the Far North rather than by his revolutionary writings, which they consider "naive and confused." They have decided that London's ideology is representative of the faulty thinking of the petty bourgeoisie.

Though Trotsky found *The Iron Heel* both stimulating and prophetic, he pointed out its greatest weakness: "The author is intentionally sparing in his use of artistic means." Even among utopian novels, a genre not noted for skillful writing, it stands out as ineptly done. The first half of the book is given over to the presentation of Ernest Everhard, the revolutionary hero, arguing with everyone in sight in order to advance his theories linking the eventual success of the proletariat with the evolutionary process discovered by Darwin. Ernest alternates between lecturing his wife, the awed daughter of a University of California physics professor, and browbeating industrialists at dinner parties and discussion clubs. He is clearly Jack London making his ideas emphatically known, winning every argument, never letting up on his opponents. When they lose their heads, he becomes even more calm, confounding them with his logic. "It was always his way to turn the point back upon an opponent, and he did it now, with a beaming brotherliness of face and utterance." Everhard, who runs into no worthy competitors in debate, puts forward all sorts of ideas from W. J. Ghent or Herbert Spencer or Karl Marx with all the assurance of an Old Testament prophet. The tone of these chapters is well illustrated by a letter which London wrote to F. I. Bamford, the president of the Oakland Ruskin Club, to which London proposed to read two chapters from the manuscript of his novel in progress. "These are new in content and are devoted to the perishing middle class, and I think it would go splendidly. Incidentally, I handle surplus value in them, and the inevitable breakdown of capitalism under the structure of profits it has reared." The two chapters read like the arguments of a high school sophomore who has just begun to explore the theories he expounds.

When action does come, it is expressed mainly through summary. Before they are driven underground, the socialists of the United States and Germany stop a world war by calling a general strike—all done in six pages; later, it takes Jack only one page to dispose of the middle class. Only in his description of the horrors of the putting-down of the Chicago commune does he become graphic and moving. Earlier much of the plot is derivative and tenuous; for instance, a great deal is made of the neglect by mill owners of a worker named Jackson who has lost his arm in an accident in handling the mill machinery. Ernest Everhard's sweetheart, who leaves the manuscript which tells the story of *The Iron Heel*, is won over to her future husband's point of view by following his suggestion that she investigate the circumstances of the accident and the abortive law suit brought by the injured worker. The whole episode, spun out by London to considerable length, is taken from a typical muckraker article by Jocelyn Lewis. Miss Lewis's workman is named Jackson, he ends up peddling rattan chairs (as he does in *The Iron Heel*), and the author, interviewing lawyers and industrialists' wives, gets exactly the same answers as does London's heroine. The article itself is unimpressive—one is never certain whether it is fiction or fact—and the fault in London's use of it lay not in his borrowing the material (he prided himself on the process of what he called "turning journalism into literature," and he listed the article in a footnote in *The Iron Heel*) but in his attempt to blow up a not untypical case of industrial mismanagement before the days of a satisfactory workmen's compensation law into an overwhelmingly serious episode indicating the complete venality of American financiers.

> —Franklin Walker, "Ideas and Action in Jack London's Fiction," in *Essays on American Literature in Honor of Jay B. Hubbell*, Clarence Gohdes, ed. (Durham: Duke University Press, 1967): pp. 262–64.

STEVEN T. DHONDT ON JOHNNY'S REBIRTH AND THE AUTOBIOGRAPHICAL ELEMENTS OF "THE APOSTATE"

[This excerpt comes from "'There Is a Good Time Coming": Jack London's Spirit of Proletarian Revolt," an article by Steven T. Dhondt. The excerpt focuses on Johnny's rebirth in "The Apostate," as well as some of the autobiographical parts of the story.]

Martin Russak, writing in the January 1929 issue of *New Masses*, called Jack London "the most popular writer of the American working class." Further explaining London's appeal to the proletariat, Russak stated that a real proletarian writer must "not only write about the working class, he must be read by the working class." And ultimately, Russak asserted, the proletarian writer's work must "burn with the spirit of revolt."

This spirit of revolt appears frequently in London's well-known socialist writings such as "The Strength of the Strong" and "The Dream of Debs." However, his appeal to the proletariat was not principally the result of such socialistic efforts. "Workers who read, read Jack London," Russak stated. "Factory workers, farm hands, seamen, miners, newsboys read him and read him again." These members of the working class easily identified with London's characters and situations because they *were* London's characters and situations. The spirit of revolt the exploited worker felt as he underwent his day's toil is the spirit of revolt he read about in London's works. ⟨. . .⟩

Jack London's early years as a victim of arduous physical labor and subservience to the overseer and factory superintendent left deep scars. The life of the factory worker was a simple one—arise before daybreak, gulp a meager breakfast, spend the daylight hours in the shadow of the machine, then fall into bed in total exhaustion. This was repeated each day of the week with the compensation being enough to eke out an existence worthy of only a sub-human animal. This life, this social injustice, is the essence of "The Apostate," the story of a boy wanting rest.

⟨. . .⟩ Johnny, although chronologically a boy in his early teens, is a hardened, mature man. He does not know the jubilance and carefree attitudes of youth. He is a machine—emotionless, cold and unmoved by such frivolity. His evening meal is spent cursing the younger children. After supper, Johnny sits down on the porch, his mind inactive. So far as his mind is concerned, it is "asleep." A machine has no mind; it has no need for thinking—it only labors.

On his sixteenth birthday Johnny advances to the loom room and at the end of three months, he is operating two looms and then, shortly after that, three and even four looms at once. He becomes the most productive of all the weavers as he approaches "the full stature of his earning power." But there is "no joyousness in life for him." He has no ideals, and but one illusion—he drinks "excellent coffee." He is a "work beast." He has "no mental life whatever. . . ."

But then, in the midst of his greatest productivity, the machine breaks down; the cogs stop turning. He comes home one evening "aware of unusual tiredness." The family is aglow with excitement—his mother has prepared floating island, an infrequently served luxury dish—but he does not even notice. "I guess I ain't hungry to-night," he mumbles, then crawls into bed, a victim of "la grippe."

During his convalescence, Johnny spends long hours on the front porch lost in "endless calculations." He keeps a pencil and paper with him as he calculates "painfully and amazingly." Each afternoon, Johnny returns to his position on the porch, but once he finishes his calculations, he sits alone

> . . . greatly absorbed in the one tree that grew across the street. He studied it for hours at a time, and was unusually interested when the wind swayed its branches and fluttered its leaves.

Earlier in the story he had been seated on the porch, but his mind had been "asleep." Now his calculations bring him a revelation, and he catches his first conscious glimpse of the tree of life. The porch has become the antithesis of what it had been previously. It now is the springboard for the activity of Johnny's mind, whereas before, it had been a refuge for complete mental inactivity.

Johnny is now nearly seventeen years old. This is, essentially, the first time in those years he has seen and enjoyed daylight. He has lived in perpetual darkness since he entered the factory, walking and returning each day by moonlight. With the discovery of daylight and the tree across the street, Johnny is being reborn, in a sense, into a world which he has not seen since infancy and innocence. It is truly a revelation for him, and he is enraptured by it.

He tells his mother the next morning that he is not going to return to the factory. "I ain't never goin' to work again," he says, and as he speaks, the tree across the street appears "with dazzling brightness on his inner vision." The tree of life beckons to him to leave the confines and restraints of a class society and to seek Eden where he can learn the real meaning of existence.

—Steven T. Dhondt, "'There Is a Good Time Coming': Jack London's Spirit of Proletarian Revolt," *Jack London Newsletter* 3, no. 1 (Jan.–April 1970): pp. 25, 26, 27–28.

⳨

JOAN D. HEDRICK ON THE DEHUMANIZATION OF JOHNNY IN "THE APOSTATE"

[This excerpt is from Joan D. Hedrick's book *Solitary Comrade: Jack London and His Work*, from the chapter entitled "London's Socialist Fiction." In this chapter, Hedrick elaborates on Johnny's dehumanization in "The Apostate."]

London describes his experience in the glass factory: "The superintendent was very proud of him, and brought visitors to look at him. In ten hours three hundred dozen bottles passed through his hands. This meant that he had attained machine-like perfection. All waste movements were eliminated." London's focus shifts from Johnny's prodigious production to the effects of this work on his body: "Every motion of his thin arms, every movement of a muscle in the thin fingers, was swift and accurate. He worked at high tension, and the result was that he grew nervous. At night his muscles twitched in his sleep, and in the daytime he could not relax and rest. He remained keyed up and his muscles continued to twitch. Also he grew sallow and his lint-cough grew worse. Then pneumonia laid hold of the feeble lungs within the contracted chest, and he lost his job in the glassworks."

Johnny's work has shaped his spirit as well as his body. He has no strong desires. Up until his apostasy, he accepts his family and his job in an uncomplaining, listless way. "His consciousness was machine consciousness" and his life is circumscribed by industrial rhythms; he goes to work when it is dark and gets out of work after dark. London writes, "In the interval, the sun has made a golden ladder of the sky, flooded the world with its gracious warmth, and dropped down and disappeared in the west behind a ragged skyline of housetops." This description of nature's beauty is given an edge by the reader's awareness that such sights are outside the bounds of Johnny's consciousness. The factory whistle, not the sun's movement through the sky, punctuates Johnny's life, just as the memorable events in his life are the minute alterations in the industrial routine—like the occasional visits of the Factory Inspector (which strike terror in the hearts of the underage boys at the machines). The most memorable event in Johnny's work life was the day he was put to work on the starcher: "It was a colossal event. Something had at last happened that could be remembered beyond a night's sleep or a week's pay-day. It marked an era. It was a machine Olympiad, a thing to date from. 'When I went to work on the starcher,' or 'after,' or 'before I went to work on the starcher,' were sentences often on his lips."

London has created a character who is almost totally the product of the machines upon which he works. He is not an actor but one who is acted upon; he has not shaped his destiny, it has shaped him—and mangled him in the process. London gives Johnny the energy to break with this dehumanizing labor, but this ending does not counterbalance the portrait London has carefully constructed of a human being who has been turned into a machine. The humanizing power of the ending is also somewhat vitiated by Johnny's limited consciousness. The break comes almost as his body's protective reaction to the pace under which he labors. He falls ill with the grippe: "All his bones ached. He ached everywhere. And in his head began the shrieking, pounding, crashing, roaring of a million looms. All space was filled with flying shuttles. They darted in and out, intricately, amongst the stars. He worked a thousand looms himself, and ever they speeded up, faster and faster, and his brain unwound, faster and faster, and became the thread that fed the thousand flying shuttles." Johnny recovers from the grippe, but the week-long rest from work that the illness afforded him changes his consciousness. He decides he will never work again. This decision appears as a symptom of insanity to his mother, who hurriedly calls the doctor again. Her main concern has been that Johnny not lose his job through this illness, and when the foreman tells her that his job will be held for him, she "anxiously" urges Johnny to thank him. The reader experiences

Johnny's refusal to work as a victory over his mother, not a victory over the oppressive system within which he labors.

London could not have described Johnny's working-class life in such convincing detail had he not experienced the same mind-and-body-destroying factory rhythm; yet London attributes to his character a consciousness more limited than his own, and this discrepancy distances London from his creation. London's detachment is apparent in his description of Johnny as he walks away from his home and his job, never to return: "He did not walk like a man. He did not look like a man. He was a travesty of the human. It was a twisted and stunted and nameless piece of life that shambled like a sickly ape, arms loose-hanging, stoop-shouldered, narrow-chested, grotesque and terrible."

> —Joan D. Hedrick, "London's Socialist Fiction," *Solitary Comrade: Jack London and His Work* (Chapel Hill: University of North Carolina Press, 1982): pp. 174–75.

⊗

JAMES I. MCCLINTOCK ON THE CONTEXT FOR LONDON'S SOCIALIST FICTION

[This excerpt is taken from the book *Jack London's Strong Truths* by James I. McClintock, specifically from the chapter "The Decline: 1906–1911." Here, McClintock discusses the context of London's socialist fiction.]

In the summer of 1906, he threw himself into the composition of his famous revolutionary novel, *The Iron Heel* (New York, 1908). At the same time, he began to compose socialist stories. Among the few socialist stories he wrote, these, in the order of their publication, are the few which still elicit interest: "The Apostate" and "A Curious Fragment" which are collected in *When God Laughs* (New York, 1911), the volume which followed *Lost Face*; "The Dream of Debs" and "The Strength of the Strong" which are collected in *The Strength of the Strong* (New York, 1914), the most widely known collection of stories with a social emphasis; and "The Mexican," collected in *The Night-Born* (New York, 1913).

The thematic break with the Alaskan stories which was entailed in writing socialist fiction is not as dramatic as one would expect; the new emphasis is a matter of degree. Early, London had emphasized comradeship as a saving element of the Malemute Kid's code, and it is a simple step from this to class solidarity. Similarly, he could turn from race theory involving a melioristic natural law to socialism's telic forces. Injustices perpetrated against Indians by gold hungry whites from civilization are like those inflicted upon "wage slaves" by their capitalist masters. This shift from individual and racial mastery to social mastery, then, is not a total departure from his earlier themes and motifs but, instead, a realignment of his ideas to effect a more optimistic view of life. He moves from the Alaskan nightmare to social ameliorization, a kind of change which Frederick Hoffman, in more general terms, believes characteristic of modern literature:

> When once the shock of violence is unaccounted for, unseen, unreal, and unreasonable, the self is separated from most doctrines of sufficient reason; it has to make its "separate peace." Since the self cannot be sustained without some viable code or some illusion, there are many contrived readjustments.

The most important unifying bonds between the Northland and socialist stories are that London could approach the different subject matter didactically and prophetically, his most comfortable authorial stance, and that both kinds of stories were justified by "scientific" theories. In the beginning of his career he hastened to find techniques to allow the presentation of "strong truths," derived in part from science; and in the socialist stories, the role of the artist as propagandist for a scientific Marxism is a recurring motif that demonstrates his messianic impulse, the sincerity of his conviction, and his continuing trust in scientific theories. ⟨. . .⟩

"The Apostate," another favorite of the critics and anthologists, is more successful than "The Dream of Debs" because it isn't ambivalent towards the working class and doesn't attempt to dramatize a complicated body of socialist ideology. In addition, it is a story of disintegration and dehumanization, contexts which characteristically had produced London's better fiction. Johnny, the "apostate," is a "work-beast" produced by a textile mill sweat shop who, as a result of the inhuman working conditions and sub-marginal wages, is ignorant, will-less, and physically misshapen. He has just enough awareness left, after brutalizing days at the machine, to realize that he is nothing more than another moving part in the machine. Without emotion, not even a hatred for the machines or a sense of bitterness, he decides to stop working. He walks out of town, lies in the grass for an afternoon and then hops a freight. Rather than a fictionalization of Marxist ideology, "The Apostate" is more a muck-raking story attacking the inadequacy of child-labor legislation and an irreverent social comment that it is preferable to be a tramp than a work beast.

—James I. McClintock, "The Decline: 1906–1911," *Jack London's Strong Truths* (East Lansing: Michigan State University Press, 1997): pp. 123–25, 128–29.

Plot Summary of
"To Build a Fire" (1908)

London wrote two versions of this story, one in 1902 and one in 1908. The first was mostly a didactic essay for the Boy Scouts on why one should not travel alone in the North. The second version of the story is the better of the two.

The man, who is never named, is traveling through the Northern wilds, alone except for a dog. He is to meet his companions at about suppertime, but he still has a whole day's journey on foot in front of him. The day is sunless, being winter when the sun does not rise, and the air is very cold. The man knows it is colder than fifty degrees below zero because at that temperature, spittle crackles on the snow. When he spits, his saliva crackles in the air before it even reaches the snow.

It is actually seventy-five degrees below zero, which means it is one hundred and seven degrees below the freezing point. The man has a beard of yellow ice from the tobacco he is chewing and spitting. His nose and cheeks are numb. He rubs them, but the minute he stops, they go immediately numb again. The dog knows that it is too cold to be traveling; its instincts tell it so. It wants the man to make a fire, for it knows that this is an ability only man possesses.

Halfway through the day, the man stops for lunch. As soon as he stops walking, his feet start to go numb, and when he takes one mitten off to build a fire, his hand goes instantly numb as well. Over the fire, he warms his feet and hands and thaws the beard of yellow ice so that he can move his mouth to eat his lunch. His lunch has been wrapped in a handkerchief against his skin to keep it from freezing.

Aside from the cold, falling into water is the greatest danger on this trip. Throughout the day, the man has been on the lookout for hidden springs. Even in the coldest weather the water does not always freeze, though the snow heaps up over it. Sometimes, the man can tell when water is ahead by the sunken look of the snow, but other times he is not sure. Several times, he makes the dog go first to test the ground. At one point, the dog breaks through, wetting his feet. This is not as great a problem for the dog as it would be for the man, but the animal immediately sits down to bite the ice chunks off its feet.

After lunch, disaster suddenly strikes. Without warning, the man falls through the snow into water, getting wet halfway to the knees. He is mostly annoyed by this, because it means a delay; he must now stop and light a fire to warm and dry his feet. He gets a little fire started without much trouble, using sticks and twigs and a bit of birch bark. His feet are completely numb from the water, and his hands are numb from having to take his mittens off to build the fire. As he is about to try and pry his frozen moccasins off to thaw his feet by the fire, something even more dreadful happens.

Without thinking, he has built the fire under a tree, where the most wood is. Now the snow-laden branches, disturbed by his plucking twigs from them, drop part of their load of snow onto his fire, putting it out. This is serious, and the man knows it.

Quickly, he gathers an armload of branches and moves out into the open to try again. His hands are so numb by now that he has lost all feeling, and he has to look to see whether he is holding the piece of birch bark. As his hands become more and more stiff, he cannot separate the matches to tear one off. Finally, he presses the whole bunch of matches between his two hands and strikes them against his leg. The seventy matches burst into flame; he smells burning flesh and then feels the pain, but he holds on until he can drop the burning matches onto the birch bark and twigs.

The bark begins to burn, and he starts to add the fuel he has gathered. Because his hands had been so numb and because he had been trying to move quickly, he had not sorted the dry material out from the green. As he adds fuel to the fire in handfuls, a piece of moss falls onto the little flames. The man tries to poke the moss out of the fire, but he is shivering violently and his hand jerks, scattering the fire across the snow. He tries to push it back together, but it is too late: the fire is out.

The man knows that he cannot light another fire. In panic, he looks at the dog and remembers a story about a man who killed a steer and crawled inside the carcass to keep warm. He thinks that if he could kill the dog, he could put his hands inside the body. He tries to call the dog to him, but it recognizes a strange note in his voice and refuses to go near him. The man realizes he could not kill the dog anyway; his hands could not hold a knife nor would they be able to strangle the dog.

Finally, in a panic, he begins to run. He thinks that maybe by running the blood will be forced back into his feet. Lacking the endurance to keep moving, however, he falls and cannot get up. He knows now that he will die, and he pictures his friends finding his body the next day. As he drifts off into a comfortable sleep, he feels warm at last.

The dog sits patiently near the man, wishing he would get up and make a fire. It has never known a man to lie like that in the snow for so long. At last the dog's desire for fire gets the better of its patience; it creeps nearer the man and whines. Suddenly, though, it smells the scent of death on the man. It stays a few minutes more and howls at the stars; then it turns and starts to trot along the trail toward the camp of the other men, where it knows it will find food and fire. ❁

List of Characters in
"To Build a Fire" (1908)

The Man is a tenderfoot, unused to the North. He is not incredibly intelligent, although he is not stupid either; he sees things quickly but not their meanings. He knows the danger of getting one's feet wet in the cold but cannot avoid falling in a hidden spring. Unable to build a steady fire, he fails to warm himself again.

The Dog is the man's only companion. It has the instincts to survive in the wild that the man lacks, but it relies on men for food and fire. When the man falls asleep in the snow, it waits patiently for several hours until it smells death on the man. It knows then that there is no use in staying and heads up the trail toward the camp. ❀

Critical Views on
"To Build a Fire" (1908)

KING HENDRICKS AND EARLE LABOR ON THE
PROTAGONIST'S HOLLOW QUALITY IN "TO BUILD A FIRE"

[This excerpt comes from an article called "Jack London's Twice-Told Tale," written by King Hendricks and Earle Labor. Hendricks and Labor here discuss the hollowness of the protagonist in "To Build a Fire"; they also compare the two versions of the story.]

What has been hinted in the beginning becomes explicit in the third paragraph, the only place in the story where the author's voice may be detected. The man lacks the one asset that might equalize the odds against him—imagination: "He was quick and alert in the things of life, but only in the things, and not in the significances. . . . Fifty degrees below zero was to him just precisely fifty degrees below zero [actually it is seventy-five below]. That there should be anything more to it than that was a thought that never entered his head." The scope of his imagination is signified in his one stock comment: "It certainly was cold," a fatally inept response that recurs with increasing irony as the man's situation deteriorates. It is also in this paragraph that the theme of the story is subtly implanted in the reader's mind: "It [the extreme cold] did not lead him to meditate upon his frailty as a creature of temperature, and upon man's frailty in general . . . and from there on it did not lead him to the conjectural field of immortality and man's place in the universe." London drops the comment so deftly that it hardly ripples in the reader's consciousness, yet it is this idea precisely that gives the story its final impact: "unaccommodated man" is indeed a frail and pitiable figure when pitted against the awful majesty of cosmic force. London expressed the thought more elaborately in one of his earlier stories ⟨"The White Silence"⟩:

> Nature has many tricks wherewith she convinces man of his finity—the ceaseless flow of the tides, the fury of the storm, the shock of the earthquake, the long roll of heaven's artillery—but the most tremendous, the most stupefying of all, is the passive phase of the White Silence. All movement ceases, the sky clears, the heavens are as brass; the slightest whisper seems sacrilege, and man becomes

timid, affrighted at the sound of his own voice. Sole speck of life journeying across the ghostly wastes of a dead world, he trembles at his audacity, realizes that his is a maggot's life, nothing more. Strange thoughts arise unsummoned, and the mystery of all things strives for utterance. And the fear of death, of God, of the universe, comes over him—the hope of the Resurrection and the Life, the yearning for immortality, the vain striving of the imprisoned essence—it is then, if ever, man walks alone with God.

But the nameless protagonist of "To Build a Fire" is unaware of these deeper implications, as we learn not only from his own behavior but also through the only other animated character in the story, the dog. The inclusion of this *ficelle* or "reflector" is the masterstroke of London's revised version. By employing the dog as foil, the author has obviated the necessity for further editorial comment. Instead of being *told* that one needs a companion in the Northland, we are made to *see* dramatically through his relationship with the animal that the man is a "loner." Because he lacks imagination, he fails to see, until too late, that a companion—even a dog—might possibly save him in a crisis; more important, he is revealed as a man lacking in essential warmth. There is no place in his cold practical philosophy for affection or for what London called elsewhere "true comradeship." To this man the dog is only another of "the things" of life, an object to be spoken to with "the sound of whip lashes." From his relationship to the animal, we may infer a broader relationship—that to mankind. The protagonist is, in other words, a hollow man whose inner coldness correlates with the enveloping outer cold. And there is a grim but poetic justice in his fate.

The dog serves as a foil in the following manner also: his natural wisdom of conduct is juxtaposed against the foolish rationality of his master's behavior. By shifting point of view from man to dog, London provides a subtle counterpointing that enhances both theme and structural tension. For example,

> The animal [unlike the man] was depressed by the tremendous cold. It knew [without the convenience of a watch] that is was no time for traveling. . . . The dog did not know anything about thermometers [which are as useless as watches if one lacks the ability to interpret]. Possibly in its brain there was no sharp consciousness of a condition of very cold such as was in the man's brain [a consciousness vitiated in the latter by stock response]. But the brute had its instinct [a surer gauge than rationality]. It experienced a vague but menacing apprehension [absent in the man, because he is without imagination]. . . .

—King Hendricks and Earle Labor, "Jack London's Twice-Told Tale,"
Studies in Short Fiction 4, no. 4 (Summer 1967): pp. 339–40.

@

SUE FINDLEY ON NATURE AS THE PROTAGONIST

[This excerpt is from Sue Findley's article "Naturalism in
'To Build a Fire.'" Here, Findley unfolds her theory that
nature is the true protagonist in this short story.]

Nature is the true protagonist in this story, man a puppet. It is no
accident that in the opening sentence the reader meets the forces of
Nature first, "Day had broken cold and gray" and man second,
"when the man turned aside from the main Yukon trail and climbed
the high earth bank." Significantly, this secondary character is never
named; he is "the man" unworthy of such distinction and
individuality as a name would impart. The second sentence
reinforces the suggestion that Nature is a power to be reckoned with:
"It was a steep bank, and he paused for breath at the top." In the
third sentence London states that "there was no sun or hint of sun,
though there was not a cloud in the sky." And again "there seemed
an intangible pall over the face of things, a subtle gloom that made
the day dark." With these economical deft strokes of the pen, the
artist gave to his readers the protagonist, a cosmos instinct with evil.

In true Freudian fashion London next set about the task of
indicating that the man was no match for the forces of Nature. The
man was lacking in imagination. "He was quick and alert in the
things of life, but only in the things, and not in the significances.
Fifty degrees below zero meant eighty-odd degrees of frost . . . that
was all. It did not lead him to meditate upon his frailty . . . and upon
man's place in the universe." By now there remains no doubt; man's
place is very minor indeed. However the man, lacking in perception
as he was, pressed forward unaware, and London made this fact
vivid with the well-chosen synocdoche, "the eager nose that thrust
itself aggressively into the frosty air."

At this point London introduced a third character, the dog, as a
link between man and Nature but identified with Nature more
closely than with man. Although it trotted at the man's heels, it was a

"proper wolf dog" and the animal knew what the dull-witted human being did not know "that it was no time for traveling. Its instinct told it a truer tale than was told to the man by man's judgment." By the time the reader has reached this juncture, the man makes a pathetically gallant figure as he "held steadily on" down the faintly marked trail at the rate of four miles an hour. Overtones of catastrophe are clear in his numb cheekbones, and in the ice muzzle of tobacco juice surrounding his mouth. He regretted without panic that he had not devised a nose strap to wear across his cheeks. This error in judgment, however, is no more than might be expected from a creature of such low degree in conflict with the evil forces of cosmic cold that "smote the unprotected tip of the planet." Note the implications in London's choice of verb. Again London reminded the reader that the dog knew it should be lying "snug in a hole in the snow" waiting for a warming "curtain of cloud to be drawn across the face of outer space whence this cold came." London did not allow his reader to forget that this cold was immense and cosmic in scope, that if the planet is dwarfed and stricken by it, man is proportionately less significant. The dog with his greater kinship to Nature was "not concerned in the welfare of the man." After breaking through the crust of ice and wetting his feet in the stream beneath, the man envied the dog as Nature's creature sat with its "wolf brush of a tail curled . . . warmly over its forefeet."

The man's struggle to build a fire in order that he might dry his footgear was unsuccessful, for Nature in a calculated move inverted the snow-laden branches to smother the last vestiges of the life-sustaining warmth. Not even that Titan Prometheus bearing his gift of fire can withstand the forces of cosmic evil. The denouement to such a mismatched contest as this between man and the universe was of course predictable from the beginning. London closed the account as it began with attention on the protagonist. Nature remained, standing exultant in its triumph. "The stars leaped and danced and shone brightly in the cold sky" when the man sat still and stiff, frozen in the cold snow. London barely managed to refrain from saying "*because* the man sat."

—Sue Findley, "Naturalism in 'To Build a Fire,'" *Jack London Newsletter* 2, no. 2 (May–Aug. 1969): pp. 46–47.

[This excerpt is taken from King Hendricks's article "Jack London: Master Craftsman of the Short Story," published in *Jack London: Essays in Criticism*, which was edited by Ray Wilson Ownbey. It was originally a Faculty Honor Lecture at Utah State University and was first published by the Faculty Association of that university. In the article, Hendricks examines the story's plot.]

The second version of "To Build a Fire" was written aboard the *Snark* in the South Seas in 1908. It is curious that aboard a small boat and in the heat and turmoil of the South Seas London would turn back to the North and write so vivid a story of a Northland tragedy and Northland irony. In this version the man is unnamed.

He was a newcomer, and consequently the white silence of the Yukon made no impression upon him. ⟨. . .⟩

He was prepared for the cold with his mittens and his moccasins, and with ear flaps and with a heavy coat and though he speculated upon the cold and found that as he spat upon the ground the spittle crackled in the air, he was unconcerned. Along with this man, and this is a difference from the first story, there trotted a big native husky wolf dog.

> The animal was depressed by the tremendous cold. It knew that it was no time for travelling. Its instinct told it a truer tale than was told to the man by the man's judgment. In reality, it was not merely colder than fifty below zero; it was colder than sixty below, than seventy below. It was seventy-five below zero. Since the freezing point is thirty-two above zero, it meant that one hundred and seven degrees of frost obtained.

The dog knew nothing about thermometers and possibly in its brain could not make a sharp distinction between 107 degrees below freezing and 101. But the dog had learned to burrow under the snow and cuddle in the warmth of it away from the air. It also had learned to appreciate fire.

As the man walked along the trail he contemplated the time of his arrival at the camp. He knew that if he maintained a certain speed he would be at Henderson Creek by 6 o'clock and would be with the boys.

He was careful as he walked on the trail not to step on certain places where the ice had barely frozen over, where he could break through and wet his feet. He knew that wetting his feet could be very dangerous. He avoided the hidden pools by noting a certain false appearance to the snow. Once he forced the dog to act as a trail breaker for him and found that the dog broke through. And after the dog had broken through by instinct it licked its legs and toes so that the ice could not form.

At mid-day the man built a fire, ate a lunch that he had carried under his coat, next to his body, and took time by the warmth of the fire to fill his pipe and have a comfortable smoke. And then he turned back to the trail. The dog was disappointed; he wanted to stay by the fire.

> This man did not know cold. Possibly all the generations of his ancestry had been ignorant of cold, of real cold, of cold one hundred and seven degrees below freezing point. But the dog knew; all its ancestry knew, and it had inherited the knowledge. And it knew that it was not good to walk abroad in such fearful cold.

During the afternoon the man inadvertently stepped on thin ice and found himself floundering in water, with his feet wet up to his knees. He knew the danger and knew that he must stop, build a fire and dry his feet and put on dry socks. He was able to start it with small twigs. He fed it very carefully.

> Gradually, as the flame grew stronger, he increased the size of the twigs with which he fed it. He squatted in the snow, pulling the twigs out from their entanglement in the brush and feeding directly to the flame. He knew there must be no failure.

Finally he felt that he was safe. The fire had been a success. The old timer had been serious in his statement that no man must travel alone in the Klondike after 50 below. Well, here he was. He had the accident, he was alone, he had kindled a fire and would save himself.

And then the unexpected happened. He had built the fire under a spruce tree which was weighted down with snow for many months, and when he pulled the twigs from the base of the tree he began an agitation, an imperceptible agitation, but enough to disturb the snow balance and bring about disaster. The snow fell from the tree upon the man and the fire, and the fire was blotted out.

With the fire gone, the man attempted to move along the trail but realized that he could not travel and attempted to build another fire. He was unsuccessful. He remembered the tale of a man caught in a blizzard who killed a steer and crawled inside the carcass and was so saved. He thought that he might kill the dog and thereby save his life. But when he spoke to the dog there was a strange note in his voice, and the dog was frightened and kept away from him. Then he tried to take to the trail again, but became weary and sat down.

Then the man drowsed off into what seemed to him the most comfortable and satisfying sleep he had ever known.

—King Hendricks, "Jack London: Master Craftsman of the Short Story," in *Jack London: Essays in Criticism*, Ray Wilson Ownbey, ed. (Santa Barbara, Calif.: Peregrine Smith, 1978): pp. 20–21. [Originally published by the Faculty Association of Utah State University.]

⊗

CHARLES E. MAY ON THE SIMPLICITY OF THE NARRATIVE

[This excerpt comes from the article "'To Build a Fire': Physical Fiction and Metaphysical Critics" by Charles E. May. Here, May elaborates on his concept of the narrative's simplicity in "To Build a Fire," while he discusses how critics have tried to make the plot more complicated than it is.]

London's central comment about the protagonist in the story itself clearly indicates the "naturalistic" nature of his Everyman: "The trouble with him was that he was without imagination. He was quick and alert in the things of life, but only in the things, and not in the significances." London says that the cold was a simple fact for the man. "It did not lead him to meditate upon his frailty as a creature of temperature, and upon man's frailty in general, able only to live within certain narrow limits of heat and cold; and from there it did not lead him to the conjectural field of immortality and man's place in the universe." If this comment "hardly ripples in the reader's consciousness," as Hendricks and Labor suggest, it is not because it is dropped so "deftly," but rather because London, like his protagonist, is without imagination in this story, because he too is concerned here only with the things of life and not with their significance. The reader may be led to meditate upon the physical limits of man's ability to live in extreme cold, but nothing in the story leads him to the metaphysical conjectural field of immortality and man's place in the universe.

James Mellard's claim that the obsessive repetitive activity in the story automatically makes it a symbolic ritual assumes that the man's repetitive activity "to build a fire" in order to preserve bodily life is equivalent to Oedipus's repetitive activity to "find the culprit" in order to find his very identity. An activity that dramatizes a biological need should not be confused with an activity that dramatizes a psychological need. And to equate the physical limitations of being unable to survive a temperature of 75 degrees below zero with the psychic limitations suggested by the Greek *hamartia* is to confuse physics with metaphysics. Moreover, to call the man's final attitude toward death, which he himself thinks of as no longer "running around like a chicken with its head cut off," an heroic facing of his fate similar to the recognition and dignity of Oedipus's final gesture is to equate heroic resolution with a simple acceptance of the inevitable.

A close look at the story itself without the lenses of *a priori* categories reveals that the most significant repetitive motif London uses to chart the man's progressive movement toward death is the gradual loss of contact between the life force of the body and the parts of the body: "The cold of space smote the unprotected tip of the planet, and he, being on that unprotected tip, received the full force of the blow. The blood of his body recoiled before it. The blood was alive, like the dog, and like the dog it wanted to hide away and cover itself up from the fearful cold. . . . The extremities were the first to feel its absence." The man realizes this more forcibly when he finds it difficult to use his fingers: "they seemed remote from his body and from him. When he touched a twig, he had to look and see whether or not he had hold of it." The separation is further emphasized when he burns the flesh of his hands without feeling the pain and when he stands and must look down to see if he is really standing. When he realizes that he is physically unable to kill the dog, he is surprised to find that he must use his eyes to find out where his hands are.

Finally, realizing that the frozen portions of his body are extending, he has a vision of himself that the story has been moving toward, a vision of the self as totally frozen body, not only without psychic life, but without physical life as well. Picturing the boys finding his body the next day, "he found himself with them, coming along the trail and looking for himself. And, still with them, he came around a turn in the trail and found himself lying in the snow. He did not belong with himself any more, for even then he was out of himself, standing with the boys and looking at himself in the snow." The discovery of self in London's story is not the significant psychic discovery of Oedipus or the Ancient Mariner, but rather the simple physical discovery that the self is body only.

—Charles E. May, "'To Build a Fire': Physical Fiction and Metaphysical Critics," *Studies in Short Fiction* 15, no. 1 (Winter 1978): pp. 22–23.

⊗

John Perry on the Circumstances behind "To Build a Fire"

[This excerpt is taken from the chapter "Snarking on the South Seas," from John Perry's book *Jack London: An American Myth*. In the chapter, Perry talks about the circumstances under which London wrote his short story "To Build a Fire."]

London had first seen Hawaii in the early 1890s, when he sailed on the *Sophie Sutherland* bound for Japan. He visited Waikiki for one day in January 1904 en route to the Orient as a Russo-Japanese War correspondent, and stopped in Honolulu on his return six months later. This time, however, members of the Hawaiian Yacht Club met the Londons, escorting the *Snark* into Pearl Harbor, where astonished reporters thought they had been lost at sea because of erroneous newspaper reports. Interviews followed. "Everybody is rated on the ship's articles in accordance with the requirements of the United States navigation laws," London answered a reporter's question. "But in practice we knew none of the distinctions between foremast hands and others. We were not only the ship's company, but we were company for each other. The trip was an ideal one, in all but speed, and as I see that a merchantman has just arrived at Honolulu twenty-five days from San Francisco, I do not see that it should be thought wonderful that we took twenty-seven. We were in no hurry. We were not like the merchantman eager to get to our destination, counting every hour as so much money, every sail full of wind as so many dollars."

During the *Snark*'s repairs, however, London did worry about so many dollars. Earlier he had counted on *The Iron Heel* for revenues to keep him afloat, but magazines wouldn't touch its revolutionary theme. The *Snark* cost $1,000 a month. California expenses also continued. What to do but keep writing. So he sat down in his kimono and completed "To Build a Fire," still his most famous short story of the freezing Klondike.

London wrote two versions of "To Build a Fire." The first appeared in the May 1902 issue of *The Youth's Companion*, a Boston-based juvenile magazine with half a million circulation. He received fifty dollars. In this earlier story, tenderfoot Tom Vincent survives, mainly because of superior human intelligence, resourcefulness, and a love of life. The tale concludes with this tacked-on moral: "In a month's time he was able to be about on his feet, although the toes were destined always after that to be very sensitive to frost. But the scars on his hands he knows he will carry to the grave. And—'Never travel alone!' he now lays down the precept of the North."

London expanded the second "To Build a Fire," evoking moods of impotence and loneliness through images of cold, deriving the story line from Jeremiah Lynch's *Three Years in the Klondike*. The hero is a frosty unnamed fellow. He's usually called a tenderfoot, someone without brute intuition or imagination who ignores the old sourdough's advice at Sulphur Creek—always travel with a companion on the trail. But this Northlander really possesses sharp insights. He studies the land's topography, its snow formations and creek changes, even forcing his dog—not a devoted canine—to scout ahead for danger spots. He falls through the ice in an area free from treacherous signs, another instance of London's gnawing pessimism and belief in an erratic universe. Both facts and logic betray the traveler in this wasteland beyond time on the world's edge, where things haven't changed for millenniums. He eventually freezes to death when snow, shaken from a tree limb, deadens his life-giving fire. *Century Magazine* published this grim tale in August 1908. "It was a weird scene; an anachronism," London had written in "The Son of the Wolf." "To the South, the nineteenth century was reeling off the few years of its last decade; here flourished man primeval, a shade removed from the pre-historic cavedweller, a forgotten fragment of the Elder world."

—John Perry, "Snarking on the South Seas," *Jack London: An American Myth* (Chicago: Nelson-Hall, 1981): pp. 226–27.

ꙮ

LEE CLARK MITCHELL ON REPETITION IN "TO BUILD A FIRE"

[This excerpt is from Lee Clark Mitchell's book *Determined Fictions: American Literary Naturalism,* from the chapter entitled "Imposing (on) Events in London's 'To Build a Fire.'" In the chapter, Mitchell deals with the story's repetition.]

Repetition establishes a compelling pattern in London's Arctic for reasons that are neither simple nor straightforward. Most obviously, its material effect is entropic, reducing the man to the purely physical by depriving him initially of a will, then of desires, and at last of life altogether. Yet it is already clear that the process manifests itself at first not in a material realm (the realm of actions involuntarily repeated) but at a verbal level. And it does so, notably, with the word most often reiterated. "Cold" occurs in the first half of this short story more than twenty-five times with a chillingly predictable effect. For just as the narrative's focus on the physically immediate contributes to a paralyzing "tyranny of things," so the repetition of a thermal absence gradually lowers the textual temperature. Or rather, the persistent emphasis on intense cold—which is no more, after all, than molecular inactivity—exposes an irreducible corporeality to the very air itself. Empty space becomes a thing.

The "tyranny of things" that develops from a repetitive concentration on the material world tends, as we have seen, to break down characteristic connections among objects as well as events. Yet repetition itself implies a more ontological stasis in terms of the story's hero, exercising its power most fully by isolating not event from event, but event from actor. The repetition of things and events creates an environment that seems to resist human intention, one in which desires fail over and over to shape results. Consequence ever falls short of anticipation, and the narrative gradually divides the man from his world by exposing the ineffectiveness of his will—not merely to reach the safety of camp by his planned time of six o'clock, but to avoid the hidden "traps" of water, then to build a warming fire, and finally to forestall the Arctic's numbing effects. The "tyranny of things" prevails over the man at first by depleting his physical resources, and at last by excluding the very possibility that he might possess any agency. As his body numbs and slowly freezes into a thing like any other thing, he apprehends in growing panic how little effect he can have on the environment. And as this occurs, we come to realize what it means for deliberate actions not to have the results we intend.

In much the same way that recurrences of plot seem to diminish a capacity for personal control (by suggesting the workings of involuntary repetition), so verbal reiterations more generally foreclose the prospects we normally assume in experience. When the man carefully builds a second fire, for instance, the warning implied by the repetitions offsets the description's calm understatement.

> This served for a foundation and prevented the young *flame* from drowning itself in the snow it otherwise would melt. The *flame* he got by touching a match to a small shred of birch bark that he took from his pocket. This burned even more readily than paper. Placing it on the foundation, he fed the young *flame* with wisps of dry grass and with the tiniest dry twigs.
> He worked slowly and carefully, keenly aware of his danger. Gradually, as the *flame* grew stronger, he increased the size of the twigs with which he fed it. He squatted in the snow, pulling the twigs out from their entanglement in the brush and feeding directly to the *flame*. He knew there must be no failure. (Emphases added)

At a purely descriptive level, the flame's repeated animation ("young flame," "flame grew stronger") lends it a life and a will of its own that refuses to be controlled by the man. Yet at a more pervasive if somewhat paradoxical verbal level, the invocation of "flame" five times in seven sentences ensures not the prospect of fiery success but rather the ephemerality of any hope. More fully confirming that effect are the fricatives proliferating through the passage, as if in partial echo of the "flame" and its predictable demise. Likewise, the reiteration shortly thereafter of the confident claim that "he was safe" establishes not the man's security but a mood of imminent peril. By translating the singular into a set, doubled language subverts linguistic authority, in the process replacing routine assurance with a mood of lingering doubt.

This verbal effect is more pronounced with words that unlike "flame" refer to capacities, not conditions. For while the narrative repetition of things makes conditions seem somehow fixed and determined, the effect of repetition on emotions and other ephemeral states of being is erosive, apparently reducing them to lower levels of possibility. Agitation or happiness or lust—simply by virtue of being redescribed in the same words—appears not simply as if less spontaneous but finally as if less real.

—Lee Clark Mitchell, "Imposing (on) Events in London's 'To Build a Fire,'" *Determined Fictions: American Literary Naturalism* (New York: Columbia University Press, 1989): pp. 39–41.

(ॐ)

James M. Mellard on Dramatic Structure and Mythical Overtones

[This excerpt is taken from an article by James M. Mellard called "Dramatic Mode and Tragic Structure in 'To Build a Fire.'" The article was published in the book *The Critical Response to Jack London*, which was edited by Susan Nuernberg, but the article was originally published in Mellard's *Four Modes: A Rhetoric of Modern Fiction*. In the article, Mellard discusses the dramatic structure and the mythical overtones in the short story "To Build a Fire."]

London creates a dramatic form in "To Build a Fire" simply by focusing upon the primary, unadorned, crucial action, the efforts of the man to build a lifesaving fire. By virtue of the trajectory, the direction of that action, moreover, London develops not just an illustrative naturalistic episode, but a truly noble tragic plot. Though focus on the objective action, the rite, ritual, or ceremony, is important, alone it is not enough to create a tragic structure. For such a structure a story must have a unified series of actions of the sort London provides in "To Build a Fire," where the minimal number of events (three) shows a rising and falling pattern in the fortune of the hero and culminates in the severest reversal of all, death itself. It is around the three fire-building scenes, then, that London develops the remaining elements of tragedy, elements that according to Aristotle are subordinate to action.

One of these is theme. London's thematic focus is upon the traditionally tragic distance between man and nature, the distance signified by man's mortality—the death toward which tragedy moves—and the distance that is not merely the province of naturalistic writers like London. Aside from the man's death, however, which necessarily comes at the end, this distance is suggested by London in the vastness of the natural setting and the man's being placed, as it were, at the apex between the natural environment and outer space itself, the point at which "The cold of space smote the unprotected tip of the planet; and he, being on that unprotected tip, received the full force of the blow."

But another tragic element is character. In tragedy, the conventional flaw of the hero is *hubris*, or pride, a mistaken conviction that one is capable of handling destructive situations more easily than he has a right to believe. London's hero, unnamed and perhaps standing for "everyman," all who must live in nature, manifests such a tragic, ultimately fatal, flaw. He flies in the face of the conventional wisdom offered by the "old-timer on Sulphur Creek," thus going against the life-preserving knowledge painfully acquired through longer, more cautious experience. After successfully making the first fire, London's hero, having thought before of the old-timer's warning about the deadly cold, thinks, "For the moment the cold of space was outwitted." And after successfully making a second fire to dry out his leggings and socks, he thinks again, even more pridefully: "The fire was a success. He was safe. He remembered the advice of the old-timer on Sulphur Creek, and smiled. The old-timer had been very serious in laying down the law that no man must travel alone in the Klondike after fifty below. Well, here he was; he had had the accident; he was alone; and he had saved himself. Those old-timers were rather womanish, some of them, he thought. All a man had to do was to keep his head, and he was all right. Any man who was a man could travel alone." But as must inevitably happen in tragedy at his moment of greatest pride he is struck down—and through his own actions. At seventy-five below zero his feet wet and hands freezing the man is forced once more to build his fire, buried now under a tree's snow avalanche, a result of his mistake in building the fire under a snow-laden spruce.

The conclusion of "To Build a Fire" now seems inevitable, the sequence of actions allowing no other end than the one London's hero senses: "The man was shocked. It was as though he had just heard his own sentence of death." Now the man knows "the old-timer on Sulphur Creek was right. If he had only had a trail mate he would have been in no danger now. The trail mate could have built the fire. Well, it was up to him to build the fire over again. . . ." But London has crafted his plot well, and we know, as well as the man, that his effort is doomed. And though London devotes several pages to the obsessive attempt to repeat the earlier performances and shows the man absolutely absorbed in his actions, all thought driven out of his mind, "devoting his whole soul to the matches," the important tragic theme that develops from the man's failure is his stoic, resolute facing of death. He has a "certain fear of death, dull and oppressive," but after manfully struggling against a force simply too powerful for his human weakness and suffering one last moment of panic, "he sat up and entertained in his mind the conception of meeting death with dignity. . . . He was bound to freeze anyway, and he might as well take it decently." He has broken a "law," he has recognized his error, and he meets his self-created fate nobly. And London leaves us at the end with death; the penalty exacted by nature; the dog, a symbol of the still mortal organism in that indifferent nature; and the natural order itself, imaged in "the stars that leaped and danced and shone brightly in the cold sky."

"To Build a Fire" recapitulates the events, if not the verbalized meaning, of a familiar *mythos*, the bringing of fire into an alien universe, the Promethean exploit that would modify nature but that would also bring death or extreme suffering to the hero himself. London touches upon this motif a number of times in the story when he reports the thoughts of the rather humanized husky—in his "instincts" he knows the man as a "fire-provider," and it is off in search of other "fire-providers" he goes at the story's end. Though there are other men who can provide fire, they are all mortal, as London's protagonist is, and they, no more than he, can ever win that battle with nature, the "god" that perpetually torments Prometheus for the theft of the symbolic flame. But these are "meanings" we must extract from London's objective presentation of acts, for these acts are depicted without much of the interpretive aid of the teller himself.

—James M. Mellard, "Dramatic Mode and Tragic Structure in 'To Build a Fire,'" in *The Critical Response to Jack London*, Susan M. Nuernberg, ed. (Westport, Conn.: Greenwood Press, 1995), pp. 19–21. [Appeared originally in *Four Modes: A Rhetoric of Modern Fiction* by James M. Mellard.]

Fiction by
Jack London

The Son of the Wolf (short stories). 1900.

The God of His Fathers (short stories). 1901.

The Cruise of the Dazzler. 1902.

A Daughter of the Snows. 1902.

Children of the Frost (short stories). 1902.

The Call of the Wild. 1903.

The Sea-Wolf. 1904.

The Faith of Men (short stories). 1904.

The Game. 1905.

Tales of the Fish Patrol (short stories). 1905.

White Fang. 1906.

Moon-Face and Other Stories (short stories). 1906.

Before Adam. 1907.

Love of Life and Other Stories (short stories). 1907.

The Iron Heel. 1908.

Martin Eden. 1909.

Burning Daylight. 1910.

Lost Face (short stories). 1910.

Adventure. 1911.

South Sea Tales (short stories). 1911.

When God Laughs and Other Stories (short stories). 1911.

The House of Pride and Other Tales of Hawaii (short stories). 1912.

Smoke Bellew (short stories). 1912.

A Son of the Sun (short stories). 1912.

The Abysmal Brute. 1913.

The Valley of the Moon. 1913.

The Night-Born (short stories). 1913.

The Mutiny of the Elsinore. 1914.

The Strength of the Strong (short stories). 1914.

The Scarlet Plague. 1915.

The Star Rover. 1915. (Published in England as *The Jacket.*)

The Little Lady of the Big House. 1916.

The Turtles of Tasman (short stories). 1916.

Jerry of the Islands. 1917.

The Human Drift (short stories and essays). 1917.

Michael, Brother of Jerry. 1917.

The Red One (short stories). 1918.

On the Makaloa Mat (short stories). 1919.

Hearts of Three. 1920.

Dutch Courage and Other Stories (short stories). 1922.

The Assassination Bureau, Ltd. (Completed by Robert Fish). 1963.

Jack London's Articles and Short Stories for the (Oakland) High School Aegis. Ed. James E. Sisson. 1971.

The Complete Short Stories of Jack London. 3 vol. Eds. Earle Labor, Robert C. Leitz III, and I. Milo Shepard. 1993.

Works about
Jack London

Ahearn, Marlie L. "'The People of the Abyss': Jack London as New Journalist." *Modern Fiction Studies* 22, no. 1 (Spring 1976): 73–83.

Allen, Mary. "The Wisdom of the Dogs: Jack London." In *Animals in American Literature*. Urbana: University of Illinois Press, 1983.

Auerbach, Jonathan. *Male Call: Becoming Jack London*. Durham, N.C.: Duke University Press, 1996.

Bamford, Georgia Loring. *The Mystery of Jack London: Some of His Friends, Also a Few Letters—A Reminiscence*. Oakland, Calif.: Georgia Loring Bamfor-Piedmont, 1931.

Beauchamp, Gorman. *Jack London*. Mercer Island, Wash.: Starmont House, 1984.

Brooks, Van Wyck. "Jack London." In *Sketches in Criticism*. New York: E. P. Dutton, 1932.

Cantwell, Robert. "Jack London: Melodrama." In *Famous American Men of Letters*. New York: Dodd, Mead & Co., 1957.

Cassuto, Leonard and Jeanne Campbell Reesman, eds. *Rereading Jack London*. Stanford, Calif.: Stanford University Press, 1996.

Clayton, Lawrence. "The Ghost Dog, a Motif in *The Call of the Wild*." *Jack London Newsletter* 5, no. 3 (Sept.–Dec. 1972): 158.

Dickey, James. Introduction to *The Call of the Wild, White Fang, and Other Stories* by Jack London. Ed. Andrew Sinclair. New York: Penguin, 1981.

Etulain, Richard W. *Jack London on the Road: The Tramp Diary and Other Hobo Writings*. Logan: Utah State University Press, 1979.

Flink, Andrew. "*Call of the Wild*—Parental Metaphor." *Jack London Newsletter* 7, no. 2 (May–Aug. 1974): 58–61.

Foner, Philip S. *Jack London, American Rebel*. New York: Citadel, 1947.

Frey, Charles. "Contradiction in *The Call of the Wild*." *Jack London Newsletter* 12, no. 1–3 (1979): 35–37.

Jaher, Frederic Cople. *Doubters and Dissenters: Cataclysmic Thought in America, 1885–1915*. New York: Free Press, 1964.

Johnston, Carolyn. *Jack London—An American Radical?* Westport, Conn.: Greenwood, 1984.

Kershaw, Alex. *Jack London: A Life.* New York: St. Martin's, 1997.

Kingman, Russ. *A Pictoral Life of Jack London.* New York: Crown, 1979.

London, Charmian. *The Book of Jack London.* New York: Century, 1921.

London, Joan. *Jack London and His Daughters.* Berkeley, Calif.: Heyday Books, 1990.

London, Joan. *Jack London and His Times: An Unconventional Biography.* New York: Doubleday, Doran and Company, 1939.

Lynn, Kenneth S. *The Dream of Success: A Study of the Modern American Imagination.* Boston: Little, Brown and Company, 1955.

Martin, Ronald E. "Jack London: Radical Individualism and Social Justice in the Universe of Force." In *American Literature and the Universe of Force.* Durham, N.C.: Duke University Press, 1981.

McClintock, James I. *White Logic: Jack London's Short Stories.* Cedar Springs, Mich.: Wolf House Books, 1976.

Nuernberg, Susan M., ed. *The Critical Response to Jack London.* Westport, Conn.: Greenwood, 1995.

O'Connor, Richard. *Jack London: A Biography.* Boston: Little, Brown and Company, 1964.

Ownbey, Ray Wilson, ed. *Jack London: Essays in Criticism.* Santa Barbara, Calif.: Peregrine Smith, 1978.

Pattee, Fred Lewis. *The Development of the American Short Story.* New York: Harper, 1923.

Payne, Edward Biron. *The Soul of Jack London.* Kingsport, Tenn.: Southern, 1933.

Reesman, Jeanne Campbell. *Jack London: A Study of the Short Fiction.* New York: Twayne, 1999.

Rideout, Walter B. *The Radical Novel in the United States 1900–1954.* Cambridge: Havard University Press, 1956.

Roden, Donald. *Jack London's "The Call of the Wild" and "White Fang."* New York: Simon and Schuster, 1965.

Rothberg, Abraham. "Land Dogs and Sea Wolves: A Jack London Dilemma." *The Massachusetts Review* 21, no. 3 (Fall 1980): 569–93.

Seelye, John. Introduction to *White Fang and The Call of the Wild* by Jack London. New York: Signet, 1991.

Sherman, Joan R. *Jack London: A Reference Guide.* Boston: G. K. Hall, 1977.

Shivers, Alfred S. "Jack London's Mate Women." *American Book Collector* 15, no. 2 (Oct. 1964): 17–21.

Sinclair, Andrew. *Jack: A Biography of Jack London.* New York: Harper and Row, 1977.

Stasz, Clarice. *American Dreamers: Charmian and Jack London.* New York: St. Martin's, 1988.

Stone, Irving. *Sailor on Horseback: The Biography of Jack London.* Cambridge: Houghton Mifflin, 1938.

Tavernier-Courbin, Jacqueline, ed. *Critical Essays on Jack London.* Boston: G. K. Hall, 1983.

Upton, Ann. "The Wolf in London's Mirror." *Jack London Newsletter* 6, no. 3 (Sept.–Dec. 1973): 111–18.

Walker, Dale. *The Alien Worlds of Jack London.* Grand Rapids, Mich.: Wolf House Books, 1973.

Walker, Franklin. *Jack London and the Klondike: The Genesis of an American Writer.* San Marino, Calif.: Huntington Library, 1966.

Ward, Susan. "Toward a Simpler Style: Jack London's Stylistic Development." *Jack London Newsletter* 11, nos. 2 and 3 (May–Dec. 1978): 71–80.

Watson, Charles N. Jr. *The Novels of Jack London: A Reappraisal.* Madison: University of Wisconsin Press, 1983.

Zirkle, Conway. *Evolution, Marxian Biology and the Social Scene.* Philadelphia: University of Pennsylvania Press, 1959.

Index of
Themes and Ideas

and death impulse, 37–39; determinism in, 9–20; and environment, 45; and feral conditions in midst of civilized human society, 47–48; Frog in, 35, 36; and Jim Hall, 47–48; Henry in, 10, 35, 36, 39, 42; and heredity, 45; and Kiche, 43, 46; and life-instinct, 37–38, 40; and love, 37, 43–44, 45, 46; and morality, 45, 46; and One-Eye, 40–42; plot summary of, 35; and Weedon Scott, 44, 46, 47–48; setting of, 39–42; She-wolf in, 10, 35, 36, 37, 38, 40; and Beauty Smith, 44, 46; and survival of the fittest, 41; and White Fang, 35, 37, 38–39, 40, 41, 43–44, 45, 46, 47; and wolf-lynx-porcupine struggle, 38, 41–42

"SON OF THE WOLF, THE," 77

"STORY OF A TYPHOON OFF THE COAST OF JAPAN," 12

"STRENGTH OF THE STRONG, THE," 56, 60

STRENGTH OF THE STRONG, THE, 60

"TO BUILD A FIRE," 63–82; characters in, 66; circumstances behind, 71, 75–77; critical views on, 9, 67–82; The Dog in, 63–65, 66, 68, 69–70, 71, 72, 73, 74, 76, 81; dramatic structure of, 79–82; The Man in, 63, 64–65, 66, 67–68, 69, 70, 71–75, 76–78, 79, 80–81; The Man's hollow quality in, 67, 69; mythical overtones in, 79–82; Nature as protagonist in, 69–70, 81; plot of, 71–75; plot summary of, 63–65; repetition in, 74, 77–79, 78; simplicity of, 73–75; versions of, 63, 68, 71, 76

"TO THE MAN ON THE TRAIL," 14

WHEN GOD LAUGHS, 60

WHITE FANG, 9, 25, 35. *See also* "SHE-WOLF, THE"